MARIJUANA
SMOKER'S
GUIDEBOOK

The Easy Way to Identify and Enjoy Marijuana Strains

MATT MERNAGH

GREEN CANDY PRESS

MARIJUANA SMOKER'S GUIDEBOOK
Published by Green Candy Press
San Francisco, CA

Copyright © 2013 Matt Mernagh

ISBN 978-1-937866-06-8

Back cover, left to right: Hindu Kush, OG Star, Trainwreck,
and White Widow.

Printed in China by Oceanic Graphic International Inc.
Massively distributed by P.G.W.

CONTENTS

CONTENTS

CONTENTS

SMOKING POT 101

I toked them all...

MATT MERNAGH

...and I probably should have known better than to attempt to write a lengthy introduction to this book after inhaling a devastating indica like Exodus Cheese. After a lengthy toking career you'd think I'd know better, but here I am, with my guide to smoking the world's best pot hung up just before hitting the press because I've chosen the wrong weed. Gawd damn! Indicas are great at managing my chronic pain levels, but they zap the creativity out of me. Unless I switch it up to a soaring creative sativa, I'm doomed to stare at a blank page, and so are you.

Marijuana and writing have been part of my daily routine for two decades. Combining the two to create a ganja guide seems like a dream writing gig until one day, you begin to struggle with words after hitting a Kush. Toking multiple Kushes and thinking creatively? Forget about it. Writing that a strain is "dank" one too many times is akin to a music critic writing, "It rocks!" for every song on an album. Just not okay.

Towards the end of this book-writing process, after sampling and reviewing hundreds of samples of amazing weed (and tending to my own my cannabis crops), I began appearing at my local pub with a 'long day at the office' look. Yes, I sampled (and smell like) five different kinds of marijuana today, but I also penned thousands of words describing the smells, tastes and effects of what I smoked. Just like any professional critic, I take my craft seriously–I reached back into my writer's bag of tricks to my days of being a young, ranting music reviewer and applied many of those techniques to the art of reviewing marijuana strains.

Instead of reviewing marijuana objectively, I completely and wholeheartedly admit to getting medicated and writing subjective reviews. Marijuana strains from the White family are my personal favorites, so I'm bound to be influenced by my adoration of White Russian, White Widow and Jean Guy. However, I love stellar soaring sativas, especially in the morning, while afternoons often bring fruity flavored hybrids and of course the well-loved Kush strains.

Can cannabis ever be reviewed objectively when there are so many variables involved in producing truly great finished bud? The same strain grown by two different people will ultimately have similar, but notably different, results. Besides using totally different methods–soil or hydro, chemical nutrients or organic plant food, etc.–there's a personal growing style that influences the way the plant grows in these different systems. In short, no two buds are truly alike.

The breeder's seeds play a significant role too, but how much? There are plenty of well-known strains available that when grown from seed produce at least two different phenotypes–groups of observable characteristics, like smell, taste and effects. Some breeders inform buyers that either of these phenotypes can appear in their

grow, while others don't. Subtle differences will create different impressions of a strain.

So when we write about pot, are we judging the strain or the grower–or both? It seems to me that the best method to examine marijuana strain is subjectively–and this doesn't mean writing, "It's super DANK" or, "This strain is FIRE, bro" a hundred and fifty times.

I toked them all and this is what I thought about them!

There's not a published article, going all the way back to my beginnings as a music geek for Exclaim Magazine, that hasn't been written while I've been under the influence of some wicked weed. That's because without cannabis I'm unable to sit comfortably in a chair and write these words. Medical marijuana allows me to function. Inhaling responsibly, I've obtained a Humber School for Writers diploma and a journalism diploma from St. Clair College, penned articles for Toronto alt-weekly NOW Magazine as well as Cannabis Culture magazine and I've made several appearances on Newstalk1010, an influential news radio station in Toronto.

Marijuana manages my fibromyalgia, scoliosis and a rare brain tumor behind my left ear better than any prescription medication on the market. I can function like a normal human with medical cannabis, whereas seizure and opiate medications render me blah. In 1997 I joined a then-fledgling organization called the Toronto Compassion Centre. It helped people to obtain high quality cannabis to treat their illnesses. When Toronto Police raided the feisty organization in 2002, I came out of the cannabis closet and began my personal quest to overgrow the government.

As the coach of a group of activists known as the Toronto Hash Mob, I've led and organized almost a decade's worth of marijuana smoke outs. We risk arrest every April 20th by publicly puffing down with friends. Now we have grown

into a sizeable crowd of thousands of tokers. Our celebra-
tory cannabis cannon (about a quarter pound in one
super-sized joint) has led to my photo being splashed in
newspapers all the way around the world. I've appeared in
print and on television numerous times in my legal medical marijuana garden. It's fair to say that cannabis has
given me a quality of life I could not have had without it.

However, it hasn't been all ganja gravy. I've been charged
for a cannabis-related offence on five separate occasions,
did two weeks in Canada's most notorious prison The
Don Jail and I've spent five of the last seven years on bail.
Yet even in these bleak moments there's some cannabis
clarity–like when a justice proclaimed during a bail hear-
ing, "That must be the largest balcony in the city", after
learning I had placed 32 plants outside to see how they
would grow 420 feet above the city of Toronto.

My so-called "confession video" (don't ever make one of these) shows me explaining to an inquiring detective, who claimed to have busted plenty of grows before but had never seen anyone label their pots, the difference between indicas, sativas and hybrids. The labels allowed me to keep track of the different strains that I confessed to growing for myself to determine which ones worked (and which ones didn't work) at treating my illness.

Turning my worst moment into my best took four years of monthly court sessions and a thirteen-day trial. Our four months of preparation, wherein lawyer Paul Lewin and I interviewed people across Canada about their inability to access the federal government's medical marijuana program, resulted in the largest victory against prohibition ever achieved. Together (myself, 22 witnesses and our lawyer Paul), we struck down Canada's marijuana laws for personal possession and growing.

I am currently the only Canadian who has a court order allowing me to possess and grow cannabis. In the last year and a half, I've grown multiple marijuana strains by a slew of reputable seed breeders and it's been a remarkable experience.

Many of the strains in this toker's guide were grown by myself or other medical marijuana users. Plenty were picked up at various medical marijuana centers from across the country and others from known quality dealers. Obtaining or growing strains wasn't a real challenge, but writing about and photographing 150 different buds turned out to be tough!

I hope that this guide will help other marijuana users to learn about the smells, tastes and effects of the most

popular and effective strains of pot that are available today. I also hope that this guide will teach marijuana users how to identify the quality and genetic nature of the cannabis that they are purchasing or growing. After all, no one likes to smoke bad shit.

How Can You Tell If You Have Stellar Weed?

If your buds are crushed and crammed into a small baggy, then they're not going to be great. Plastics degrade cannabis. Static cling in the baggy can pull precious trichomes off the buds and on to the plastic walls of your baggies. A sticky bag is terrible news for a smoker, because by the time you get at the bud, all that ganja goodness has gone to waste. To avoid this, keep your buds in a small glass jar that seals in the pot's freshness.

Marijuana doesn't naturally come compressed in bricks, nor is it crumbly or broken up in pieces. Buds should be attractive to the point of being pornographic to potheads. Your first thoughts when encountering stellar weed should be, "I can't wait to roll you up and toke you all night long."

Great ganja is gorgeous because its trichomes sparkle. The red, green and sometimes purple hues are majestic and the leafy material has been properly manicured. Properly cured buds are dense, firm and, most importantly, easy to grind. Once ground, all that remains is a sweet, sticky, and resinous mound of marijuana.

Besides being pretty, stellar nugs have a noticeable stink. Some will have a more noticeable stench than others, but all should have a smell. When busted, each particular marijuana strain's unique aroma will become very noticeable. I've had some strains that, after getting busted, released a smell that made my mouth water.

How To Tell Quickly If Your Dealer Is Selling Great Ganja Or Bunk Bud

Don't buy your bud on a street corner. Instead, develop a trusted nug network. Develop a reputation for having dank nugs and you will soon discover that your access to amazing strains increases. Potheads who have great ganja like sticking together because it makes the session that much more stoney.

Regardless of all the other arguments, marijuana should be legal simply because phoning half a dozen people on a Friday night seeking some pot to get stoned with is just wrong. How many calls of, "You got any trees?" do you have to make before marijuana legalization just makes sense? Plenty of people have a regular hook up, but even that person might not truly be worthy of their business.

Did your weed come pre-packaged or in small dime bags? Then it's bunk for sure. Avoid the dealer who has everything pre-arranged and packaged. A reputable seller will weigh out their wares on a scale in front of you and be very proud of their product. Many will be very boastful of their buds. Stick to your regular hook up when buying large amounts, and when purchasing from some-one new, buy less to test their product and reputation.

Just because your guy says he's stocking "the Kush" doesn't mean it really is "the Kush". Stay cautious of the person who says they have super bomb strain x-y-z, but why not give them the benefit of the doubt, especially if it's awesome pot and matches up with this guide?

How To Tell If Your Marijuana Has Mold

Contrary to popular fear mongering, mold will not kill you, but still, you should never consume cannabis that you know is moldy. For prohibitionists, mold is the new blob; a magical and deadly monster that no one can see or knows much about, but which can kill unsuspecting teens. However, in reality, mold is just a problem created by moisture lock.

Marijuana Smoker's Guidebook

When moist marijuana is packed in airtight containers the conditions to create mold are perfect. Most growers cure their cannabis correctly, but when they don't, consumers get moldy products.

Be on the lookout for a white stringy substance that clings to buds around the stems. If you spot something that doesn't look like marijuana plant matter then it probably isn't. Bust open the suspected area and more white gunk should be apparent. Some mold appears as black spots on your buds, but I've found the most common to be a white mildew-like substance that clearly is not cannabis. Discard any affected plant matter immediately and be thankful that shit isn't in your lungs.

How To Tell If Your Marijuana Has Been Sprayed For Taste Or Weight

Some professional potheads are known to lightly lick their bud at the base of the stem to determine if it's been sprayed to improve taste and weight. Some growers and dealers will spray sugary or salty solutions on to their bud to make it weigh more, and therefore make more money off it. Beware of this ganja garbage. It's out there. When smoking tasty sprayed weed you're going to notice an unreal or flavored rolling paper or blunt wrap-like taste—especially if you're vaporizing. Experienced heads will know instantly that it's not natural and it doesn't take much for you to know either. Dealers spraying cannabis for taste and weight should be frog marched to city hall and put in stocks to be publicly ridiculed by potheads everywhere.

How To Tell If You Have An Indica or Sativa Before You Smoke It

If it looks like the Kush, it's probably an indica. Determining if it's an indica or a sativa before toking a strain is a huge cannabis challenge. Hybrids have made characteristics between indicas and sativas very blurred. It's much easier to tell the difference between indica and sativa when they're still growing because the characteristics are more pronounced in the living plant.

However, most of the marijuana you'll come across will be an indica-dominant hybrid that creates a sedate kind of stone. This is because most cultivators agree that indicas are easier to grow and are faster finishing. Generally speaking, indicas are fatter, denser and smell less exotic. Most indicas won't stink up a room when the stash jar is open. Sativas are leaner looking and can be slightly wispy but will stink up a room real good when grown correctly. Remember that because hybrids have become so commonplace, the best way to tell is to sample the weed.

How To Moderate Your Cannabis Consumption

Good luck with that. When you have fantastic cannabis, moderating how much you're toking can be a challenge. However, staff at a BYOB (bring your own bud) lounge

Marijuana Smoker's Guidebook

12

called Vapor Central sometimes do
have to clean up puke after tokers
have over indulged. Generally
speaking, alcohol plays a role, but
not always. Sometimes–and it is
very rare, thankfully–people do get
so stoned that they vomit.

New potheads especially can easily get overwhelmed on
weed, but that's part of the fun. Remember that you're not
going to die. It's best to take deep breaths, drink some
juice and make yourself comfortable because your setting
plays an important role in the experience. Stoners have
been known to leave Vapor Central much more ripped
than they thought after getting up from a couch and going
outside because their setting has changed. Take things
easy and slow, and don't run for the hills!

Take the time to enjoy your cannabis. Inhale some then
kick back and wait for the effects before going further.
On nights when you're going full bud bore, put out a variety of munchies in advance to keep yourself well fed.
Try to avoid just the junk food, too.

Experienced folks should never put new tokers one toke
over the line intentionally as that's just bad form–we are
classy cannabis lovers over here, after all. It's not a
reefer race nor is inhaling the most marijuana some
kind of cannabis contest. Our foremost goal is to derive
the maximum enjoyment and benefits from our ganja.

How To Tell If You've Got Indoor Or Outdoor Grown Grass

In my experience, I have seen that indoor trichomes are

fatter and more plump, whereas outdoor weed is more hairy and rough looking. Outdoor cannabis has a rougher appearance than indoor cannabis because it's been subject to harsher conditions. I've been accused of babying my marijuana plants in my indoor grow room because I once adjusted a fan speed after a friend decided it was "a little too low." Who does that? Come on!

How To Tell If You Have Organically Or Chemically Fed Marijuana

Unless you grow it yourself or know the grower personally, finding organic marijuana can be a real cannabis challenge. Some medical marijuana centers offer organically grown grass, but few do. Even Amsterdam coffeeshops don't have much in the way of bio cannabis. Most cannabis will be fed some kind of chemical nutrient and then flushed of these nutrients in the final weeks of flowering. Growing organically has become much easier, but I doubt commercial growers are going to change their methods from using chemical plant foods. Regard-

less, it's all in how the cannabis has been flushed. Poorly flushed organic marijuana is going to produce results that are just as bad. Your marijuana should leave behind a nice white ash in your bowl or ashtray if it's free from the nasty shit.

How To Tell How Potent Your Cannabis Is

Smoke it, duh! On first inspection you might have potent pot if it is sticky with resin, packed with glittering trichomes and dusted with cannabis crystals. Stinky cannabis can also be a sign that you're about to get higher than the proverbial kite. However, even the most beautiful buds can be a huge disappointment when you smoke them. Some strains given advance hype never live up to their reputation for potency. Use the wise weed words of others, but don't just rely on the name of the nug to determine its potency.

Advice For My Medical Marijuana Friends

Accessing a variety of affordable strains is exceedingly important when medicating with marijuana. To receive the most benefit from med buds, patients need to know what they're medicating with. Various strains provide different effects and some may provide better relief than others, but other than strong anecdotal evidence we don't know much about how certain strains affect various ailments. Contrary to what some people may pitch to medical patients, every cannabis strain affects people differently and you need to experiment in order to determine what kind of pot is best for alleviating your symptoms.

I'm wary of recommending one strain over another because the ultimate benefactor is the breeder and what works for me might not work for you. There's an honest statement! Medical marijuana center staff can, of course, direct their patients to specific strains based on the reports of patients with similar afflictions. However, I'm not sure if this really extends beyond their own medical marijuana menu. Given the subtle nuances of growing cannabis, patients need to learn to recognize not only the strains that help their condition but also the growers and production methods that produce the cannabis that they prefer. Knowledge is power.

White strains work for my fibromyalgia because they provide pain relief without making me sleepy. I'm not sure if there's something extra special in these strains or if I get a really pleasant placebo effect. Either way, it doesn't really matter because ultimately I'm getting the symptom relief that I need.

The goal of medical marijuana patients is symptom relief and we don't really require anything more than anecdotal evidence for our own personal medical marijuana discoveries. My guide mentions many strains that are effective for pain relief and I hope that it can work for many as a starting point on their journey towards being a ganja guru capable of identifying and enjoying great marijuana.

ACKNOWLEDGMENTS

Hash Mob Honor Roll

Christina Moorshead, Erin & Chris Goodwin, Mann, Mark Klokeid, Matt Oliver, Sean Brady, Paul Lewin (and The 22 witnesses in R v. Mernagh), Sita Windheim, Tracy Curley, Adam Glover, Daniel Boughen, Martin Legabbe, Heather Parry, Dave Unrau, Eric Compton, Adam Greenblatt, Dana Larsen, Jeremiah Vandermeer, Michael Mage, Steve "Wanna A Dab Matt?" Hunter, Sarah Sunday, Jillian Hollander, The Weedy Guy, Amy Anonymous, Bud Cannibus, Compton, Potato Pipe, Jack Draack, Yoda, Montreal Martin, Opus420, and The Potheads Who Don't Smoke Schwag, Head Shop Canada, iMedikate, Toronto Compassion Centre, Cannabis As Living Medicine, Rainbow Medicinal Cannabis, Green Harvest, Pixel Dreams, The Jim Richards Show (and Britt), Cannabis Culture and of course Vapor Central.

ACAPULCO GOLD

Along with Skunk #1 and Northern Lights, Acapulco Gold
was one of the first consistently popular marijuana
strains. You can still find these strains, but they're no
longer imported like they were "back in the day." Seasoned tokers who experienced Acapulco Gold in their
youth may tear up or experience an emotional flashback
when toking these nugs. During the '70s Acapulco Gold
was imported from Mexico, but my sample of this zippy
soaring sativa arrived from growers in Canada's prairie
province, Saskatchewan. The alert, active high is well balanced with a wonderful body relaxation experience.
However, too much of a sativa strain like Acapulco Gold
can make some people paranoid. The high of this strain is
a slow ride upwards, which makes it a great social stone
and because it's not a fast acting sativa it won't cause too
much jitteriness after a session. After blazing a joint or
doing a bong rip, you might want to get stuff done around
your home or go outside and enjoy the day. You can for
sure count on not sitting around or even sitting still.

ACID

Some enthusiasts avoid poorly branded strains such as
Acid on pothead principal. I'm not sure why it's labeled
after an hallucinogen, but some people dislike Acid for
the same reasons that they dislike Green Crack. Paradise
Seeds' Acid doesn't have much of a trippy effect or
aroma, but it does have an explosive scorching taste. A
fuel-like flavor from the Diesel parentage rolls over your
taste buds something fierce. It's not as fuel-tinged as
ChemDawg or NYC Diesel, but Acid does have a powerful bite. The chunky buds are light green with pinkish

trichomes and produce a rich, dense vapor or smoke.
You should anticipate an uplifting happy high. People
suffering from depression will love its positive vibe, as
Acid is truly mood enhancing marijuana that will put a
perma-grin on your face for a considerable length of
time. Just sit back and smile.

AFGHANI

These gooey buds are bursting with robust earth tones. Afghani nugs will be loaded down with heavenly smooth flavors, but will cause a cough ranging somewhere from a lung tickle to a harsh hack. Afghani is an exceedingly sticky strain that creates especially messy joints. Resin dripped out of my joint and ran into the palm of my hand; a small river of orange goo. Obviously, due to this, Afghani is an ideal hash maker. Recreational and medical smokers will really love its powerful narcotic effect, as it has an incredible amount of pain relieving properties that brought my pain levels down dramatically. However, it did leave me cloudy-headed or, if you like, stoned to the bone. Afghani is best before bed or on days when the pain is off the charts and you have nothing else to do but kick back and be gunned on ganja all day. The resinous, hashish-flavored Afghani buds create a powerful full body stone that plants you deep into the earth. You're going to put roots down in your session space. I know I did.

AFGHANI BULLRIDER

A west coast legend, Afghani Bullrider would be loved by enthusiasts if they could find it as easily as Kush. Dense AB buds will not release their beautiful silken hashish aroma until busted, but then they stink up a room something fierce with an exceedingly pleasant exotic, erotic smell. Afghani Bullrider produces an awesome and extravagant hardy toke. The flavor has plenty of depth to it, and its smooth, earthy tones blend perfectly with the hash-y taste. Afghani Bullrider pain relief is top notch without too much of a mental thud. I didn't lose my mental focus after a session. It made sitting in a chair much easier to the point where I was glued to my office chair happily getting tasks done. It is an excellent couch-locker with long lasting effects, stellar taste, stone and aroma.

ALIEN DAWG

Alien Dawg is a heavy indica without much distinguishable odor. The Cali Connection has bred their landrace Afghani (referred to as Alien Technology) with Chem-Dawg, and the stone definitely takes after the Afghani, providing a very sedate, heavy, couch-locking indica effect. Its lack of smell can be easily overlooked because it has a deadly taste and buzz. If you're lucky you will catch a whiff of a flat, earthy Afghani aroma, but don't be surprised if you don't smell anything at all. The smoke starts out very hash-y, then becomes an acidic bite. The wonderful Chem-style bite lingers while you're comfortably numb; exactly what you would expect given its ganja genetics. This makes Alien Dawg a great choice for people with chronic pain problems. The sleepy quality is wonderful late at night, meaning this strain has two fantastic medicinal marijuana traits. Alien Dawg's taste is purely from the ChemDawg lineage, and combined with the effects, it's perfect for an after dinner, "got-nothing-to-do-but-kick-back-and-unwind-after-a-difficult-day" session. Resistance to its overpowering downward effects will be futile. It's totally toking out of this world.

ALIEN KUSH

Alien Kush's toke must be from another planet. Kush genetics have been treated with some extraterrestrial wizardry to create this stoner standout. It has a wonderful down-to-earth taste and a vibe that is somewhere between Hindu Kush and Purple Kush. Anticipate spacing out for a few hours and losing track of time, just as if you've been abducted. It's Alien Kush's best feature: suddenly you're jolted from your spaciness wondering where the last two or three hours went. Did I just sit here staring off at the walls listening to my own voice or did aliens beam me up to their fantastical spaceship and test my cannabinoid levels? Before now, sightings have mainly been along Cali's west coast, but now Alien Kush is starting to get spotted in the rest of North America, too. In the words of Fox Mulder, "I want to believe!"

AMBROSIA

The combination of many cannabis strains in a single joint is commonly referred to as a salad, and Ambrosia truly is a stoner salad. It's an equal balance between God Bud, an indica and a Burmese sativa, with an aroma leaning more towards God Bud – so much so that the first toke got me thinking I'd picked up some God Bud nugs. Ambrosia is a relaxing, clear headed, thought-provoking kind of toke, and video gamers report that Ambrosia is fantastic for long online sessions. Fascinatingly, I found my second vapor bag to be much more flavorful, dense and astonishing than the first. The beyond solid Ambrosia nugs have an incredible heft to them and should make a plopping sound on the scale when weighed. Ambrosia is wonderful weed with enough couch-lock and alertness to keep potheads pleased while playing.

AMSTERDAM CHEESE

There are a growing number of cannabis Cheese varieties, with all of them gaining much love for their pungent, astringent aromas. According to folklore, the original Cheese was discovered in a pack of Sensi Seeds' Skunk #1. Due to its unique flavor it was kept as a clone only – slowly growing more and more legendary – until seed breeders began to offer their own versions. Amsterdam Cheese, with its softer tastes than the original Cheese, more closely resembles UK Cheese than Exodus Cheese. I acquired all three during the same strain hunt to create my own Cheese-y comparisons. Amsterdam Cheese is easier on your taste buds and the buzz doesn't last as long as the UK or Exodus varieties. It's a moderate indica stone, but nothing spectacular. There's some noticeable mild and mellow effects, but professionals will not be impressed. The aggressive taste is spot on Cheese, but kind of generic – like a watered down example of UK Cheese. Amsterdam Cheese is the spray cheese of these strains – the generic or "no name" brand of the Cheese varieties. Seek something more exotic when it comes to Cheeses.

APOLLO 11

You'll be able to really distinguish Apollo 11 from the smells wafting from her. The aroma is soft lemon, but doesn't explode into a beautiful stink when busted, which is kind of disappointing. Apollo 11 is a zippy "get-up-and-go" booster rocket of energy that is great for your morning wake and bake. However, it's not a smooth buzz, but a distracting, hard to focus weed wallop. Too much will for sure send you on a space-y trip beyond the moon. Unlike other sativa strains with their wonder-ful flavors, there's little noticeable in the taste depart-ment here, making it a challenge in a blind toker taste test. However, it does have an awesome, long lasting flight. Apollo 11 buds should be incredibly dense, glis-tening with crystals and specked with little red hairs. The strain appears and grows like an indica, but the buzz is all sativa. An awesome choice for sativa lovers if high is more important than taste.

APOLLO SNOW

A delightfully unique smelling strain, especially for an indica, Apollo Snow has everything that professional pot-heads seek in a stone. The smell is loud and proud with a Cinderella 99-esque flavor that's more than impressive. These two traits and the appearance of the curiously compact buds may confuse some tokers into believing Apollo Snow is a soaring space-y sativa, but it isn't. Well... it kind of is. The buzz is very physically grounding while your mind becomes intensely introspective. After inhaling Apollo Snow you might even find yourself watching paint dry because a doobie of this strain will have you daydreaming all day long. It's really easy to lose track of time after a session and only when Apollo Snow's long lasting stone wears down will you discover that your mind has been floating in space for hours.

ATOMIC HAZE

When pummeled by your grinder, Atomic Haze releases a surprising and spicy berrylicious aroma that is
similar to Northern Lights #5. I was thrown off a little
when I busted the light, fluffy buds for my morning session, thinking someone slipped me an indica instead of
a sativa, but it was fantastic for my wake and bake.
Atomic Haze is loaded with a mental get-up-and-go, but
also has a strong couch-locking sensation that is difficult to break out of. The soaring, creative high is a fascinating combination of the heady Haze and relaxed
Northern Lights. There's nothing worse than getting all
paranoid and jittery after toking a joint and Haze strains
are known for their paranoia – especially when too
much is inhaled. Thankfully Atomic Haze has a nice
calming stone to go with its explosive mental zing that
means you won't be pacing around or running up the
walls after puffing down on a joint.

BC MANGO

Even before you spark up your BC Mango nugs, you'll notice that the weedy, fruity aromas wafting from these dense, indica-looking buds smell incredibly delicious. BC Mango has an overwhelming fruity scent and reddish trichome development. The marijuana mango scents are rich, potent and intense and when breaking up the dense buds tokers will become totally tantalized. On BC Mango's first rip, potheads fall in love. The lofty but grounded high has plenty of creative, uplifting pop to it and much can be accomplished when BC Mango is used for a wake and bake session. When you're finished you should have an energetic "get-'er-done" attitude that will last throughout your day. The uppity buzz also improves moods, so I would suggest that people who have depression issues or are just suffering a day of the blues should consider some expertly grown BC Mango.

BERRY CRAZE

Who isn't crazy for a fruity, blueberry-flavored cannabis strain? Before Kush took over, potheads were all about fruit flavored strains. Now it can be difficult for the average enthusiast to find fruity tokes because of all the Kushes, which is sad because Berry Craze has a commanding "bowlful-of-berries" flavor that taste tokers will quickly twig on to. This strain looks like it was soaked in cannabis crystals and the peaceful, smooth elevation is perfect for soaking up sunshine. Berry Craze puts a spring in your step, but not a jog. Plan a wonderful sunny-day doobie with a bowl full of fruit to experience what I'm talking about. Berry Craze complements a fruity snack perfectly. Unfortunately, it's a private head stash making it almost impossible to find unless you have the right hook up.

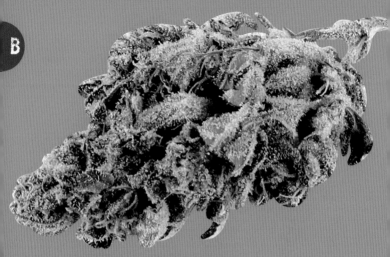

BIG BUDDHA CHEESE

This strain just reeks of Cheese-y cannabis. Big Buddha's Cheese is unreal and sets a great standard to compare other Cheese strains to. Both this strain and Green House Seeds' Exodus Cheese have an incredible aggressive flavor and a stone that puts most Kush weed to shame. You won't have many problems distinguishing upper crust Cheese strains as their stink will give you away in public at 100 paces unless you're in the supermarket's dairy aisle. Big Buddha's Cheese will glue your ass down and potentially have you sliding out of the chair. Toke in a recliner for best effect! Noobs and professionals alike may green out on its out-of-this-world buzz. The really relaxing stone is great for slow, lazy afternoons. Big Buddha Cheese is part of a growing number of Cheese strains that tokers really twig to.

BLACK DOMINA

This Afghani-hashish-meets-black-licorice flavor is an incredibly unique aroma that needs to be experienced to be fully understood. Black Domina exudes an exquisite and exotic vibe that puts it a cut above almost everything else. Once you've experienced this, you're going to want to find it again and again – or even better, grow it yourself. The true Domina is a stoner standout in the categories of aroma, flavor and stone, with an incredibly yummy aniseed flavor that your taste buds will remember long after it's gone. This strain tastes and smells so good, I could toke it all day. However, if you smoke for long, you will become unproductive quickly. It's exceedingly difficult to write about Black Domina and vape it at same time, but I tried. This strain sits your ass down and won't let it go for several hours. Your ability to communicate may dampen and friends could overstay their weedy welcome simply because they can't move. "I better go now or I won't be able to go home for hours," one colleague said, as he politely excused himself after a session. A sedate stone puts plenty of people to sleep, either for an afternoon weed nap or straight through until morning. It's a stellar pain reliever, especially for chronic joint pain. Black Domina is a cannabis classic, a great alternative to the Kush ganja glut, and relatively unknown.

BLACKBERRY

Interestingly, there's a noticeable, harsh Blackberry tang on the exhale of this strain, but not on the inhale. When busted, Blackberry nugs will release a considerably dark, fruity smell; it's a very tasty toke that creates slow sluggish vibes. During the day it's probably best to counteract the powerful indica properties with some caffeine or a sativa or you'll find yourself napping. When combined with one of these more "uppy" options, Blackberry becomes the perfect pot for wake and bakes because you'll get a speedy but relaxing effect. Beware: without a stimulant, the downward relaxing buzz will lock you up and this could potentially get your day going very slowly. Blackberry is clearly an evening toke for after everything is done or perhaps a daytime smoke for people with chronic pain problems. A great strain to vaporize before bed.

BLUE HAWAIIAN

Gorgeous, sparkly and covered in trichomes, Blue Hawaiian has a slightly tropical taste that meshes perfectly with its berry fruitiness. The buds are so pretty you might want to pause to admire before busting them – but don't pause for too long! It has an exotic flavor that goes down smooth and exhales easy; I was able to take deep, heavy rips of Blue Hawaiian with no problems at all. Anticipate a sedate and mentally stalling stone. Blue Hawaiian really fogged up my brain good, making it a challenge to do these weedy write ups. Potheads will love Blue Hawaiian's great stress relieving effects: your woes disappear after a session. For optimum results put your favorite chill music on beforehand. There's nothing worse than getting comfortably high and forgetting to put on your perfect pothead music. Tunes just sound better after blazing Blue Hawaiian because it enhances your senses.

BLUE SATELLITE

This soaring, blue-berry scented Spice of Life strain releases a rich, expressive berry aroma when ground up. The confusing smell means that Blue Satellite can easily be mistaken for straight up Blueberry. However, the Blue Satellite taste and effect is much different from DJ Short's most famous strain. Blue Satellite produces a tasty, flavorful toke with an austere after bite, which is rather surprising for a fruity strain. Nugs will be heavily dusted with trichomes, ensuring that a little amount goes a long way: half a Volcano vaporizer canister created several London fog bags. It's a much smoother ride than straight up Blueberry, and smooth slow rides are best when taking it easy. You can kick back with Blue Satellite because it creates one of those introspective zone outs; the kind of head-space where you find yourself in a peaceful zen state, staring blankly at walls, thinking or trying to think about absolutely nothing. Blue Satellite will send you on a wonderful trip around the planet and even the boldest sativa lover will spend a considerable time in orbit. The flight starts out fast until reaching your personal orbiting space, and then you'll be coasting at your perfect high for a long time.

BLUE WIDOW

This wonderful spicy Blueberry and White Widow mix has excellent aromas, flavors and most importantly an awesome mental pep. Blue Widow buds are just popping with unique, fruity White strain smells which become even louder after busting. Potheads who experience its rich, opulent flavors will remember this one even after a serious heady session. Blue Widow has motivating, uplifting and mildly body relaxing properties. It's excellent wake and bake weed and great to toke throughout the day, but I'd avoid it at night because you won't be sleepy at all. The strain produces an awesome thick and dense smoke that's not aggressive. Blue Widow is soft, mellow, tasty and easy to inhale with a flavor that's going to last until the end of your session.

BLUEBERRY

The marvelous marijuana fruitiness created by DJ Short's Blueberry set a standard by which all berry strains are now judged. Blueberry is the main ganja genetic building block of dozens of berry-flavored cannabis types; somewhere in almost every berry strain lurks a Blueberry. The original has a delicious, frothy, berry aroma, flavor and high. Just a little nug produces an incredibly yummy, berry-licious tasting vapor bag, and smokers should anticipate sticky, gluey ganja joints. Blueberry has both a soaring lofty feeling and a body relaxing mellowness. A nice, slow, upward ride. The best thing is that this vibe has plenty of legs! However, there's something about Blueberry that makes it difficult to judge how far gone you are, until you're straight up jittery – or at least that's the case for me. It's not a comfortable feeling, and it eventually fades away. If you go over the top, just ride it out with deep breaths, not 911 calls. It might be Blueberry's outrageous taste that keeps me toking more than I should. Sadly, with so many berry hybrids available these days, it's a little more challenging to find the real Blueberry.

BLUEBERRY HASHPLANT

Every time I toke Blueberry Hashplant my creative energy is zapped because it's mostly an indica with a dull,
downward stone, leaving me nothing more than a sluggish thinker. This berry-delicious indica has wonderful
body relaxing qualities and is perfect for unwinding a
stressed out mind. Don't anticipate accomplishing much
after a session. The stone keeps going-and-going-and-
going, probably until you're sleeping comfortably. Yes, it
does taste like blueberry tinged hash! The gutsy hashish
taste of Hash Plant meshes perfectly with Blueberry's
fruity zeal. The parents produce buds that have great
bag appeal, but the nugs didn't have much smell to
them. I'm surprised this one isn't around more—or more
available from a reputable seed breeder for mass con-
sumption. It's kind of surprising given the genetics are
both very solid and readily available. Blueberry Hashplant is worthy of this kind of attention.

BLUEBERRY HAZE

This strain is a potent, spicy, fruity offspring of Blueberry and Haze that has a slight hint of berry aromas when first whiffed, though it's not very noticeable compared to other fruity strains. Once inhaled you'll taste the berries instantly, but be more prepared for an astringent after-taste: a spicy shock! The stone leans more towards indica than sativa, providing a relaxing body buzz with a space-y, euphoric mental zing. However, tasty Blueberry Haze is a creeper high, making it easy to overindulge. The underlining Haze can create a paranoid mind state if too much is inhaled; you may find yourself dizzy, stressed or overly worried. The idea is to get an enjoyable zip on, not a panicky freak out. Approach Blueberry Haze with cannabis caution because it'll easily send you over the moon before you know it. Anticipate a long-lasting, soaring skyscraper effect and you'll be fine. This strain is not newcomer friendly; however, it's perfect for a personal, professional pothead's head stash.

BLUEBERRY KUSH

There was an overwhelming stench of fresh blueberries coming off these buds and the accompanying Kush odor danked up my place something fierce. Blueberry Kush is damn yummy with smooth Blueberry flavors giving way to heavy Kush overtones that hang on your palette. The buds have plenty of ganja girth to them, but they're easy to break up. This marijuana strain produces an excellent and hardy vapor bag and a resinous joint. Blueberry Kush is a lung tickler with wonderful in-the-zone vibes that are perfect for mental activities; whether you're playing chess or video games or making art, this strain will bring your game to the next level. After a session you'll become very focused and task oriented. My video gaming was much improved after Blueberry Kush and it was great for book editing.

BLUEBERRY OG KUSH

Two classic types of cannabis combine in this strain to create one stellar stone. Blueberry OG Kush is a tasty indica with subtle hints of berries hiding behind a wall of pure Kush zest. The stronger OG Kush zing simply outshines Blueberry in this combination, creating an awesome pain reliever with a sedate, mellow, focused but active effect. Chronics who play video games will love the bullet time effect that Blueberry OG Kush creates. One joint or a vapor session makes it easy to get in the zone. I love playing video games that allow for many toke breaks with cut scenes, and Blueberry OG Kush made gaming for hours so enjoyable – possibly *too* enjoyable. The buds produced a harsh heavy vapor that caused some coughing, but many Kushes do that to me. Blueberry OG Kush is a stupendous strain, but not as readily available as it ought to be.

BUBBA KUSH

Renowned for its incredibly rich, exotic flavors, Bubba Kush is one of the premier Kush strains. This is a standout amongst the crowded Kush cannabis field with its over-the-top smell, though its buzz and taste are very worthy too. Bubba Kush, after Purple Kush and Master Kush, is on the top of just about every pothead's toker taste test list, especially if they're a Kush fanatic—and who doesn't adore Kush? Bubba Kush has been around for some time, with plenty of people offering their own take on this excellent toke. Anticipate dense fluffy nugs, potentially with flecks of purple because Bubba Kush bag appeal is top notch. When busted, buds will dank up your room with serious Kush odors so beware you don't get busted by the man. The difficult to disguise smell will notify neighbors both nosy and marijuana loving. Bubba Kush is a gorgeous indica strain with plenty of slow-you-down, body numbing, pain relieving properties. The stone is intensely relaxing, long-lasting and sleep inducing. Basically, it's everything you want in a Kush.

BUBBLE ASSAULT

This beautiful smelling blend of AK47 and Blueberry is a delightful combination of these two cannabis classics. The AK47 really shines through with its strong scent when the buds are first busted, but it's the dash of Blueberry that makes Bubble Assault unique. Buds produce a rich, resinous vapor that produces a hardy pothead lung-tickling cough. Billed as an even split between indica and sativa, Bubble Assault slowed me down, but not completely. Great for getting household tasks completed, video gaming or spending time in your grow room. Bubble Assault very much resembles classic mid 90s cannabis in look and feel. Until now, Calgary, AB wasn't known for marijuana, but with this creation, Crazy Diamond Seeds has made at least one critic take notice.

BUBBLEGUM

The wonderful sweetness really shines on once Bubble Gum is busted. A sticky, syrupy smell just wafts off the rolling tray. There are many examples of this type of sickly sweet aromatic cannabis that I like to refer to as 'Memories of Amsterdam'. The dark red and green colors really make Bubble Gum pop, so much so that you might consider for a moment not busting it up, but once you do, it has an incredible introspective high and body relaxing qualities making it wonderful weed to come home to at the end of the day. After rolling a doobie of Bubble Gum, kick back in your favorite easy chair and let the stress roll off you. When you close your eyes and set the mood you'll enjoy the effects even more.

CANNALOPE HAZE

I'm all about a serving of fruit first thing in the morning!
While Cannalope Haze doesn't technically qualify, it's
still utterly fantastic for morning sessions. This straight
up sativa from DNA Genetics has a nice accessible
melon flavor, and the soft, supple smell is delicious.
Cannalope Haze is really easy to inhale. One reason that
it's perfect for wake and bakes is that it has no harsh
cough, making it easier on your lungs in the morning.
You're going to be flying on an easy take off, as this
sativa gives a soaring, motivational, "get it done" flight.
Be prepared to knock tasks off your to do list! The all-
natural, get-up-and-go high is preferred by many potheads over caffeine beverages; why choose Red Bull
when you can inhale Cannalope Haze and enjoy its
weedy wings? A morning serving will help many enthusiasts through their whole day, or at least until 4:20pm.
Unfortunately, Cannalope Haze is fairly difficult to find
unless you know a grower or have access to a well
stocked, sativa loving dispensary. With people seeking
motivational marijuana, Cannalope Haze may become
more available, at least on dispensary menus.

CATARACT KUSH

When it comes to really buzzed, glued to the couch or heavily pain relieved, Cataract Kush goes above and beyond the call of doobie. The Kush taste is unbelievably smooth, yummy and delicious, impressing even the hardest of Kush-hating snobs. People with chronic pain really enjoy Cataract Kush's stellar flavor, which doesn't wear thin even when you constantly toke it. Even seasoned stoners have problems keeping their eyelids from becoming heavy or getting flushed red and squinty. Some stoners refer to this as Visine weed. Cataract Kush is a powerful indica cross of LA Confidential and OG Kush that creates excellent long-lasting body relief. Unless you want a weed nap, I'd suggest rolling half your regular size joints. Hardy bong hitters should be prepared for a huge, lung expanding experience. This is truly "if you don't cough you don't get off" weed.

Marijuana Smoker's Guidebook

C

CHAMPAGNE

Why doesn't this bud go down smooth like the alcoholic beverage it's named after? It doesn't even have a tingly, bubbly taste. I don't get it. Shockingly, the toke has a fairly rough pine forest taste, which takes some getting used to. I personally like it, as it reminds me of Northern Lights with its harsh, juniper tones. The earthy pine smells explode when the nug is busted, and the high creates a moderately sedate and relaxing vibe. Champagne is excellent wake and bake weed, because it's rather weak. You can smoke a joint or rip a bong load before heading out the door to start your day fairly gunned, but not useless. The light chill effect should keep you going until lunch hour. Champagne's rough and hardy but unimpressive looking buds have a classic '70s look to them. This isn't the prettiest pot, especially considering its name.

CHEESE

Cheese strains are an acquired taste; some tokers have turned their nose up at this stinky, burnt-cheese-smelling offering, especially when the buds smell like goat or foot cheese. However, Cheese is becoming a very popular strain with a cool origin story. It's not for the faint at heart, or people with lactose intolerance. According to legend, Cheese was discovered in a pack of Sensi Seeds Skunk #1. Recognizing its uniqueness, the grower kept some clones; skip ahead a few years and now almost every seed bank has their own version. The bud smell is extremely noticeable before busting, becoming even stronger after they've been broken up. Most Cheese strains lean more towards indica than sativa, but all have the recognizable Cheese odor. This sample had a nice downward thump with an alert mental zing. The soaring uplift is smooth not jittery. Unlike some Cheese samples that have an awful goat cheese smell, this one was pleasant and aromatic. It was expressive without the yucky stench that turns some stoners off.

CHEESE CAKE

A growing variety of Cheese strains are becoming more readily available for discerning potheads. Like the actual dairy product, it comes in all forms; from harsh, hard flavors to soft delicate ones. Unlike some of the other kinds of Cheese cannabis out there, Cheese Cake's taste is soft, enjoyable and lights up your palate. Anticipate a strong, sensational aftertaste that is going to linger on your tongue long after your joint has been roached. Cheese Cake is a smooth, soaring sativa with awesome clarity; your flight will be very focused. Nugs are incredibly dense and upon first inspection it will appear like an indica. Actually, the only way to tell it's a sativa is to inhale. Cheese Cake is heavy and delicious like the dessert, but not quite as fattening, so you can go back for seconds and thirds without feeling guilty.

CHEMDAWG

The energetic, insightful and mood elevating effects of ChemDawg are sometimes overlooked because everyone who experiences its unique, metallic tinge can do nothing but talk about its taste. However, its soar is equally as strong. Potheads talk and talk about Chem-Dawg's jet fuel-like flavor after they've inhaled it. The strain is very similar to New York City Diesel or Sour Diesel making it very easy to get these three strains confused, but this is sour, yucky-face marijuana at its best. The unreal tart taste is not for every toker, but those who do enjoy metallic sourness will really want to discover ChemDawg. Not until they're ground up do the big fluffy buds release their unnatural pollution smell; it's an overpowering chemically stench that easily fills a room. ChemDawg has a restful, alert buzz that isn't typical of a sativa. There's no jittery paranoia if you toke too much, and instead you seem to get into a great groove.

CHERRY x AK-47

Kind of like adding cherry syrup to Coke, the Serious
Seeds cannabis classic AK-47 receives a little pop in the
flavor department. Cherry is a very welcome fruity sensation and is perfect for plumping up the rather bland
tasting AK-47. The clean, fruity aroma jumps when
busted and a small amount will create a serious session.
Anticipate a chewy, candied cherry taste with a slamming astringent after bite. The high is social and mentally alert, with a humming body buzz. The strain is
labeled sativa dominant, but many enthusiasts will be
fooled into believing its smooth, relaxing, unwinding
high is an indica. The AK-47 bud structure remains:
heavy, yet slightly fluffy. Cherry x AK-47 isn't an official
release, but it should be. Sadly, as this is mainly a private
stash, picking some up is difficult, but finding AK-47 is
not. In the mean time, there's no need to create your own
cannabis genetics; simply add a tasty Cherry sample to
an AK-47 joint to experience a similar effect.

CHOCOLATE THAI

Czart! The rich dark chocolate and coffee aroma wafting from Chocolate Thai will bring any pothead to their knees. The airy, foxtailed nugs are absolutely unreal! When it comes to smells this one is by far one of my favorites; it smells so good it may trick you into toking it all at once. However, it's best not to be like a kid devouring their first stash of chocolate or there could be some serious consequences, such as an inability to focus or sit still – much like a kid on a sugar high! Chocolate Thai is über-potent, which can easily create sativa panic attacks, freak outs and other pot paranoia. If this happens, just remember: you are not going to die! Relaxing might be a problem, but you will not shuffle off this mortal coil. Take deep breaths. The zip of this strain is akin to Mario bouncing around the clouds, but finding some Chocolate Thai is as difficult as beating Bowser – at least for me. Given its lengthy flowering time, grow challenges and wispy exceedingly light buds, not many growers choose Chocolate Thai, making this fantastic cannabis exceedingly rare.

CHOCOLOPE

Rocking out at 95 percent sativa, DNA Genetics' Chocolope is a sativa lover's dream – and, in fact, a cannabis
lover's dream in general. It's a gorgeous old school
strain with a soaring flight time and tasty cocoa
cannabis tang. Chocolope grabs potheads harder than a
kid pulling their mom towards a candy store. Stoners
who were on the scene in the '70s and '80s may experience some kind of Thai fantasy flashback. I wasn't inhaling then, so I don't know, but I do have friends from
those days who dig their sativas. Chocolope harks back
to the day when Thai cannabis ruled the roost with its
uplifting, motivating high and its taste of bitter ground
coffee and chocolate-y awesomeness. Toke with caution,
as its brightly green and red colored small nugs produce a powerful, potent and heady high that can lead to
pothead paranoia. This is jittery, fast paced marijuana.
Think of it as an espresso shot of pot.

CHRONIC

With a name like Chronic, this strain has to be utterly amazing. Serious Seeds' juniper-scented offering has been around for some time, and has become a true cannabis classic by anyone's standards. The Northern Lights-like fragrance is subtle, but still fairly strong for an indica that was first released in the mid-90s and then updated in the 2000s. It's been a long time since I've heard stoners refer to cannabis as "chronic"; back in the day potheads used to say they have "chronic" like enthusiasts say they have "kush" now. It wasn't a reference to this specific strain, but just great weed. Chronic has a distinct but subtle, delicious flavor, and the smoke is so heavy you can chew on it. The buzz is an excellent balance between relaxation of the body and mental alertness: a very chilled experience and great for productive afternoon sessions. Chronic will probably couch-lock new tokers, but seasoned and professional potheads will enjoy going about their day after a session. Chronic is a charming cannabis strain and is readily available because of its appeal to commercial growers.

CHRONIC RYDER

This autoflowering cross of Chronic and Lowryder offered by The Joint Doctor demonstrates their dedication to producing excellent boutique strains. Despite it being an autoflowering strain, Chronic Ryder's potency, aroma and flavor stays fairly true to the much larger Serious Seeds classic. The beautiful, dense nugs have amazing bag appeal and will make a "thunk" sound when dropped on your rolling tray. The buds have a mild juniper smell, but really stink like Chronic after you grind them up. You can't chew Chronic Ryder's smoke like you can with Chronic, as the Lowryder smooths out Chronic's harsher elements for a much easier toke. It's still a really rich smoke, but just isn't quite as lung expanding. The stone is spot on body relaxing, but not overly sedate, making it perfect pot for my pained mornings. Unfortunately, Chronic Ryder is a small producer, meaning that it is usually only available for people who grow it and their lucky friends.

CINDERELLA 99

Cinderella 99 has a fantastic bitter smell. When the buds are broken up they release an even more amazing sourish, fruity aroma which is more like fake or factory created grapefruit than real acidic grapefruit, akin to the taste of Sour Patch Kids. Weird, I know! The euphoric, uplifting weed whir is wonderful for wake and bake sessions and is great at relieving stress. Cinderella 99 helps me get through a mountain of chores. If Monday had an official marijuana strain, Cinderella 99 would be a good choice because it can create ganja giggle fits but not put you totally out of commission. Too much will give you coffee-like jitters, and there is also a possibility of some paranoia. The buds are especially dense, considering it's more sativa than indica. The best method to determine whether your stash of Cinderella 99 leans more towards sativa or indica is to smoke it.

CINDY 99

Cindy 99 has the familiar grapefruit smell of Cinderella 99, but the effect is dramatically different. That's because Cindy 99 is an indica, whereas Cinderella 99 can lean either way. The stone, scent and flavor are much more muted than Cinderella 99. Cindy 99 puts your mind in a sleeper hold and shouldn't be toked before going out, unless you're planning on doing a very slow moving activity. Before going out to a party, I sparked a phatty of Cindy 99 and had to hit my bed instead of the scene. It's easy to overindulge on this powerful indica, with consequences such as missed social engagements because of long peaceful sleeps. Instead of an acidic aftertaste, the flavor is very smooth and sweet. Goes down very easy.

CRIPPLE CREEK

Cripple Creek is a uniquely named (think The Band song, or the Neil Young classic) commercial Kush cross. It has wonderfully relaxing properties, just like a slow winding creek. The incredibly dense and compact buds create a very long lasting buzz and it takes just a few nugs to really have an enjoyable experience. This strain gives great Kush value for your dollars! When busted, the buds release a strong harsh Kush smell that could be either Pine Tar Kush or Cocoa Kush, depending on who you sourced it from. Prepare your taste buds for a harsh beating as this is an aggressive tasting toke. Cripple Creek is a Kush lover's delight, mostly because it is affordable and has a heavy downward stone. This weed seriously wallops you! It's not suitable for an afternoon session and don't even attempt a morning session. Though I did try hard not to take a nap after an afternoon vapor session, Cripple Creek won. There's nothing wrong with getting canna-crippled to the point of needing a weed nap, and this strain is perfect for that.

C

Marijuana Smoker's Guidebook

CRITICAL +

Be prepared to lose track of time after toking this weed.
The heavy indica of Dinafem Seeds' Critical +, a Big
Bud/Skunk cross, creates strong relaxing vibes. You just
sink into your chair, not quite locked into it, but at one
with your furniture. Hours may go by before you realize
you've been mellowed all afternoon. The headspace is
very meditative for both mind and body. Actually, Critical + is a difficult strain to perform creative tasks on and
errands too. The smoke is extremely strong and ganja
gutsy, producing a heavy vapor bag. Many people will
cough, especially when Critical + is ripped in a bong or
possibly even a joint. The smell is minimal and the flavor
leans heavily towards a harsh Skunk. I'm a fan of Critical
+ and prefer this sort of Skunk flavor over the sweetly
sickly Skunk taste that so many other Skunk strains have
going for them. Unless you're intending on napping, inhaling Critical + during the day is not advisable.

CRITICAL HAZE

The gorgeous aromas of perfume that come from Critical Haze are pretty, but are not so girlish that they're a toker turn off. Some of the Critical + strains have this Amsterdam scent to them that is a little too much for me, but I'll continue to toke them to see if I can acquire a taste for them. Surprisingly for a sativa rooted in Haze, the buds of Critical Haze have a solid girth to them. The tender red trichome hairs are classic sativa and as such, Critical Haze has a very trippy high that turned me into a stoner space cadet. Critical Haze's light, zippy and not too spicy taste is fantastic and will light up your stoner senses. Bong-ripping professionals are for sure going to notice a spicy Haze flavor. The stone goes straight to your eyeballs so anticipate heavy lids and the sort of red eyes you can't explain away by saying that you have a cold.

CRITICAL YUMBOLT

An incredibly yummy combination of Yumbolt and Critical +, this cannabis strain is a powerful and potent pain reliever as well as a sedate couch-locker. At first glance its bland looks are kind of deceiving, but Critical Yumbolt is weed worth checking out. The nugs are hardy, rough hewn and mildly ugly, but pack a potent indica punch. What its buds lack in beauty, Critical Yumbolt makes up for in a killer body buzz. I highly recommend this one for pain relief because it cut mine in half on a day when I was practically in tears from chronic pain from my head right to the tip of my toes. About half a Volcano vaporizer canister produced several rich, heavy vapor bags of pain relief and the smoke was great for curling up into bed and sleeping. That's weird for weed that leans more sativa than indica, but that's what happened to me.

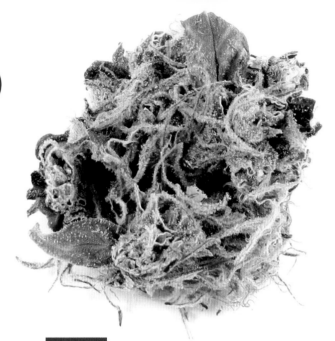

CRUSH

Crush buds are packed with plenty of delicate red trichomes so be sure not to crush your stash when hiding it. These little red hairs are extremely fragile and will cling to plastic bags via static electricity like kids cling to their parents on the first day of school. Instead of inhaling its greatness, you're then stuck with crushed trichomes, making the baggy all sticky. For a sativa, the strain has very little noticeable flavor and smell. Major pothead points are deducted for no smell sativas, making this strain mid range at best. However, Crush did produce an excellent and rich vapor bag of mostly uplifting giddiness, but my flight time wasn't a long haul. Instead, Crush created a quick uplifting jolt, but with a quick end time, leaving me with not much to write about.

CRYSTAL MOON

One would expect Crystal Moon to be packed with glittery trichomes, but it's not, leaving me baffled over the reference. Nevertheless, the plentiful red trichomes mashed into the green buds create pretty indica nugs with fast acting but short-term pain relieving qualities. Crystal Moon worked wonders on my scoliosis pain. The strain creates a sedate lazy high, but not a nappy stone. I felt very grounded, with an unexpected mental clarity. I was expecting a space-y orbiting effect, but there wasn't one. The buds gave off a bland Northern Lights-like smell. The boring aroma lacked a lively tone and the flavor was barely noticeable. This private stash got me gunned, but lacked anything else worthy of doing another session with it.

DEADHEAD KUSH

Just a small nug of Deadhead Kush will have stoners blocks away showing up at your door; it is by far one of the stinkiest Kushes around. Imagine the Grateful Dead playing in your backyard. It's not safe to travel with Deadhead Kush, especially on public transit. People will start sniffing themselves and the air to find who danks. It happened to me and it could easily happen to you. The rock hard buds produce an expensive, heavy Kush-flavored smoke that will cause plenty of cannabis enthusiasts to cough up a lung or two. This is strictly a nighttime toke because its powerful sedative properties will put even the hardest of professional potheads down for a weed nap. One regular-sized doobie dropped my pain levels in half. I can understand why this is a popular medical strain at dispensaries. Deadhead Kush's effects are long lasting and only a little is required to get even the most tolerant tokers beyond blazed.

DEEP PURPLE

As you might expect, there are some seriously heavy
grape and purple flavors to Deep Purple. This becomes
very noticeable should you take a moment to inhale its
gorgeous scent before ripping, vaping or rolling a joint.
The grape-y scents are so very impressive that they really deserve your extra attention. Deep Purple is an indica dominant strain which is an excellent balance of
Purple Urkle and Querkle (which sounds like a kids' TV
show to me). About halfway through my session I found
myself slipping and sliding out of my chair because
Deep Purple has amazing body relaxing
effects; it's rare that an indica can
put me so solidly down for
the count, but this one
did. Tired and weary
weed warriors will re-
ally twig to Deep Pur-
ple because it knocks
you over completely.
This strain made me
want to sleep for
hours, and after a few
vape bags, I did just that.

EXODUS CHEESE

Exodus Cheese has a reputation for a pungent, rancid, mountain goat cheese dank and a lazy stone that hits you right behind your eyeballs. The funky stench is extremely astringent and so God awful overpowering that many potheads will for sure make some kind of disgusted face. Exodus Cheese buds are exceedingly chunky, but when cured correctly will break up beautifully. This indica dominant strain stands out for its couch-locking, slack jawed, full body melt. My first time experiencing a stellar sample in a bong had me sliding out of my chair ten minutes later. That hasn't happened to me in a long time, and people around me were amazed. It's like the first time you inhaled! For many people Exodus Cheese induces a serious munchies attack too. Some stoners may find themselves sleepily eating cereal or other easy-to-access foods as Exodus Cheese makes you very lazy. Have your necessary supplies nearby because it's long-lasting, with a trip being around a four hour haul. Exodus Cheese is a stellar example of not just Cheese varieties, but ganja in general.

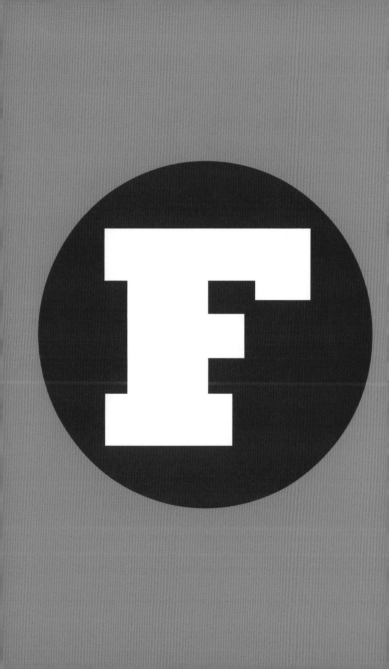

F

FRUIT DEFENDU

A somewhat lively, fruity smelling strain, Fruit Defendu is a rugged tasting toke capable of toppling over many professional potheads. The hefty, solid, almost commercial looking nugs are kind of off putting, but don't let that stop you from trying this strain. Fruit Defendu is an incredibly potent indica that dropped my pain levels numerous notches. Medical marijuana people will love that just a little goes a long way in producing great effects. Professional potheads will truly enjoy its stoned out vibe and the fact that it is wonderful weed for kicking back in a recliner. Fruit Defendu has a long lasting buzz with lots of potential for napping after a session. Make yourself comfortable in advance with the necessary technology and toke-ology nearby because you're not going anywhere after inhaling.

GRAND DADDY PURPLE

It's unfortunate that my Grand Daddy Purple sample
didn't have the purple hues it's supposed to have. I
sought out a better sample, but alas, I couldn't find one.
Deep shades of purple are one way to tell if you have
the real doobie deal. However, GDP doesn't always turn
purple, making it a challenge sometimes to determine
its true identity. Grand Daddy Purple has a great Purple
Urkle grape flavor and smell to it. The big, dense buds
create a fantastic, heady, relaxing rush with a good
amount of laziness thrown in. The lazy vibe is really fun
for playing around on Facebook, Twitter, Tumblr or
wherever you may e-roam. Grand Daddy Purple is more
mass-produced (and therefore readily available) on the
west coast than on the east coast where it remains more
of a boutique-style bud.

GRAPE GOD

Grape God is a stellar hybrid of two beautiful strains:
God Bud with its excellent exotic earthy aromas and
powerful stone and Grapefruit, famous for its tart taste
and uplifting zip. It's best to prepare your toker taste
buds for a smooth but aggressive acidic bite. The hefty
buds have an incredible overwhelming rich grape
scent. Overpowering fruity sensations lean more towards tangy grape rather than a sweet grape. Grape
God's concentrated smoke and vapor made me cough
like a nug noob with every inhale. It's a very challenging
strain on my lungs and bong rips bring tears to my eyes.
Grape God is a popular indica at many medical dispensaries. This strain possesses a fantastic body relaxing effect without any loss of mental clarity. Some people may
find that Grape God has a nice stress relieving effect
too. Like God Bud, the buzz begins to build into a
cannabis crescendo and can continue to get stronger
and louder the more you toke.

GRAPE GOD KUSH

These lush, rich purple buds are exceedingly distinct, allowing Grape God Kush to stand out in the crowded purple cannabis field. This strain possesses a flavor that is aggressively grape-like, with heavy earthy Kush and purple candy qualities creating a remarkable tasting toke. Experienced heads will recognize three unique features that build upon each other; Grapefruit's grape, God Bud's smooth resinous taste and Purple Kush's purple candy. Grape God Kush has a wonderful couch-locking, pain relieving, sedate mood enhancing vibe. It's the kind of strain that you can't wait to come home to. Not much is going to get done after hitting a bong or joint's worth of this powerful indica. Novices will be put down for the cannabis count and marijuana reviewers will have problems writing words. Grape God Kush zapped my creative energy and made me want to nap something fierce when I sampled some to write this entry.

GRAPEFRUIT

This is an easy one to figure because of its fabulous, appetizing, fruity aroma that is pure pink grapefruit. The overwhelming Grapefruit zing is just as amazing. When inhaled, it's slightly acidic, just like the fruit it's named after. Each mouthful feels like you're drinking a glass of grapefruit juice. Just a little nug produced wonderful amounts of dense, flavorful vapor. Best of all, Grapefruit didn't lose its concentrated taste after multiple vapor bags. The edgy taste complements its soaring zip, which gave me a serious case of morning munchies. Buds are loud, compact and sparkle under natural lighting. When cured correctly, Grapefruit nugs break up beautifully. Everything about this strain makes it perfect for breakfast, from its fruitiness and aroma to its smooth stone. You're going to know if you have the real deal because Grapefruit cannot be faked. There are several versions of Grapefruit, but the acidic grapefruit smell is a dead giveaway.

G

GRAPEFRUIT DIESEL

A very tart strain that is a serious lung tickler, Grapefruit Diesel's delicious sour taste had me hacking like a noob. The coughing comes from exhaling because your taste buds are still trying to recover from the inhale tartness. Best of all is the fact that this strain doesn't lose its flavor after successive vapor rounds. Grapefruit Diesel is a soaring sativa with plenty of mental clarity. I suggest making a to-do list before rolling a doobie because it's really easy to check off tasks after toking. Gamers should note that it's perfect pot for a round of Xbox or PS3 because its effect is speedy and focused. It's fairly easy to tell that Grapefruit Diesel is a sativa upon quick inspection because the buds are fluffy, but not wispy.

GREAT WHITE SHARK

Anticipate an aggressive, lemony, almost acidic stench that isn't released until after Great White Shark's solid glistening buds are busted. Your nose is going to be bitten by its strong, astringent aroma. Depending on when the strain is harvested, Great White Shark can be a more heady high or a heavier body stone; it leans more towards indica when picked early and more towards sativa if picked later. Regardless of this, it's a fab daytime toker with an uplifting "get it done" vibe. Developed in 1997, this strain has become well known and plenty of seed breeders offer their own version of this cannabis classic. However, GWS is waning in popularity making it not as readily available as it once was. I really have to have Great White Shark for Discovery Channel's Shark Week, and, like sharks, these buds are becoming fewer and fewer. There's something about toking Great White Shark and watching sharks that's just so, well, stoner.

G

GREEN CRACK

Stupid stoner naming or simple toker truthing? Some people don't like the branding of this bud, but I'm not overly offended. Green Crack has a fruity, earthy aroma that's not overpowering, but not too subtle either. It's a strong sativa, but it's not the most potent pot I've ever inhaled, and I've sampled numerous offerings. Green Crack has an incredible flight time. It gets you up quickly and keeps you there for a while, depending on your tolerance level. The high is all jumpy with little ceiling. Green Crack is another offshoot of Skunk #1, existing as clone only for some time. As its lore grew, demand for seeds became heavy, and breeders eventually crossed it with an unknown indica to smooth out an uplifting sativa zip. Buds have a soft, loose structure with plenty of trichomes and heft.

I think the name Green Crack complements its unreal zippy effects. Though it's not deadly, the buzz can certainly disorient people.

GREEN HARVEST

Not to be confused with the makers of the PollenMaster, Green Harvest is a rough looking, chunky, sensational sativa that produces fantastic smoke. The aroma is very inviting. Green Harvest is an accessible, bright smelling strain, but doesn't look like one because the buds are really fugly. This shouldn't be used as a judgement to determine potency: ugly nugs can be awesome too. Green Harvest has a motivational, happy high with plenty of get-up-and-go, go, go! Even the most sluggish person will be happily bopping along in their chair. It's not a straight shot up, but a nice smooth ride with plenty of chill body relaxation. The moderate pain relief is an added bonus. Everything about Green Harvest makes it wonderful morning marijuana.

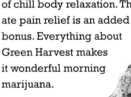

Marijuana Smoker's Guidebook

HEADBAND

Ganja God damn! Headband is a rich hardy toke that will make your eyes droopy and your lungs ache. Everything about Headband is heavy, including its bud structure and earthy bouquet. The smell isn't Headband's strong point, but that's easily overlooked by a stone that will ground you for hours. Headband has excellent pain relieving properties, making it great for people with chronic pain issues. Enthusiasts will love its slow effect and even the hardiest of potheads will toke out if inhaling too much. This is choice cannabis for before bed. Headband is extremely delicious with a zesty, sour zing, which makes it exactly the type of cannabis you're going to want to inhale often. The buds have awesome bag appeal; they're just gorgeous! They are incredibly impenetrable and sparkle with trichomes. Everyone loves very sparkly nugs that break up beautifully. A little amount of bud produces plentiful results, making it more than worthwhile financially. Reserva Privada Headband, also known as Sour Kush, is a combination of some stellar genetics as it brings together Sour Diesel and OG Kush. Parental genetics are not always a sure sign the offspring is going to be ganja good, but it does help to have awesome lineage.

HEALTH CANADA

Talk about a stoner score! Only people legally allowed to grow cannabis have access to Health Canada's marijuana seeds. My bud buddy Montreal Martin and I met in Vancouver where we discussed ganja genetics. One toke lead to another and he convinced himself to grow Health Canada's medical marijuana seeds because no one I knew had done it before. At a meeting in Toronto he gifted me with his result: a nug of Health Canada ganja he grew organically. The plant is really ugly, he says, but produces impressive looking but small buds. This is proof that any ganja grown well can produce stunning results. Health Canada's seeds are some kind of old school hardy Afghani indica with a powerful peppery toker taste; you could season a steak with its peppery zeal. The pain relieving properties were excellent and it grounded me beautifully. People will appreciate its nice, slow, sedate stone if they can get through its overbearing peppery taste.

Marijuana Smoker's Guidebook

HINDU KUSH

Harsh, chewy and rough-hewn, Hindu Kush continues to be a stand out strain amongst a crowded Kush field. The powerfully potent indica has everything Kush lovers talk about. Scoring high marks as an originator to the Kush craze with a rich exotic taste, Hindu Kush has flavors that ride down a smooth silk road before expanding in your lungs. It's one of those strains that coined the toker term: "if you don't cough you don't get off." The strain is a cannabis classic that can be enjoyed by newcomers and old-timers alike, especially now, because there's so much Kush that, going back to the original, I wanted to use it as a ganja gauge. Hindu Kush is still one of my all time top favorites. When I revisited, I tweeted a note to myself about re-membering to grow some Hindu Kush beans in the future. You should do the same!

HONEY BEE

The sweet, succulent smells from Honey Bee will really get your stoner senses tingling. An almost pure sativa with a wonderful weedy scent of earth and honey, it has a surprisingly heavy, rich and dense toke for an uplifting euphoric high. These gorgeous buds will brighten anyone's day – especially after they're inhaled! Honey Bee creates a very happy buzz and a mental alertness that probably makes it perfect pot for people with depression or stress issues. My physical stress began to disappear completely with my muscles becoming much more relaxed after a session. The tension in my upper back lessened dramatically and I was able to do some stretches. Honey Bee sure is a hard worker when it comes to keeping you high and happy.

ICE CREAM

When you spark up these nugs, anticipate a rich, creamy cannabis flavor that truly is akin to eating an ice cream cone. Savvy stoners should seek out this strain's small hints of vanilla flavors when taking a deep inhale. It's best to use clean toker utensils to get the best out of the smoke and to appreciate the strong piney taste riding overtop of these vanilla tones. Many enthusiasts will also smell sandalwood or incense. Ice Cream nugs are not soft at all; they have an incredible robust heft to them. This is beautiful, classic, chunky monkey weed with bright, bold red hairs. After a session, you'll most likely experience feelings of mental relaxation and some wonderful, mellow, meditative qualities. This great calming effect is just like the one you get from eating comfort food.

I

ICE KUSH

The zesty, Kushy goodness from Ice Kush is going to linger on your toker taste buds long after the joint has finished its rounds. It's not aggressive, harsh tasting or rough on your lungs, but may cause some potheads to cough. Ice Kush is a hardy toke that produces luscious, thick vapor and smoke. A resinous and sticky strain, but the buds will easily break up beautifully. Solid nugs that look just like Hindu Kush cover up the slick Durban Poison high that comes out to play 20 minutes after inhaling. Ice Kush is a fantastic hybrid because it starts out as a slow and steady sedate stone but ends on a zippy high. However, the couch-lock and laziness makes it a real cannabis challenge to do anything more than hanging out on Twitter, Instagram, Facebook and YouTube.

ISLAND SWEET SKUNK

Though Island Sweet Skunk appears and hits just like an indica, it's a savory, mostly sativa strain. For people who associate the smell of Skunk with weed, this strain is the perfect pot. Skunk lovers are going to love smelling their ISS stash, which has a fairly rancid, sickly sweet Skunk stink – although I've never understood associating sweetness with Skunk. When you encounter an actual skunk you don't think, "what a nice sweet aroma; I'd like to inhale more." Island Sweet Skunk tastes especially robust when ripped in a bong. The first vapor bag is amazing, but I did notice a considerable drop in the second. Island Sweet Skunk's complex flavors are best described as sugary and musky, and can be an acquired toker taste. The smoke is rather expansive and heavy, and after a session it made me feel kind of lazy; not tired, but not motivated to do much. I felt like a lump. This is wonderful weed for movie watching or doing something relaxing without much thinking involved.

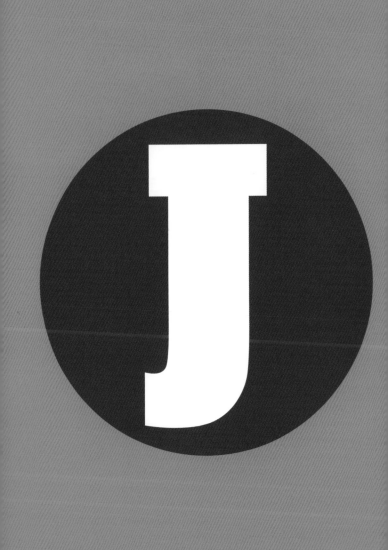

JACK FLASH

A complex, woody smelling cannabis capable of producing expressive flavorful tokes, Jack Flash has a very muted or closed aroma. Even after busting some buds, you might not smell it. Upon closer examination Jack Flash will have you thinking it has to be an indica; heavy dense buds with beautiful, delicate red hairs. Only when you get halfway through your session do you begin to realize it's not an indica, but instead a very heady high. Jack Flash has an extravagant, clear-headed high that's both talkative and social. It's great party weed because potheads will start to wax poetically, politically or even incoherently. There's nothing better than doobie discussions before, after and during a session.

JACK HERER

The alluringly lively, spicy Haze smells comprising Sensi Seeds' Jack Herer marijuana strain are some of its strongest traits. This is a powerful smelling and potent, soaring sativa with a fantastic indica side to smooth out its zip. Jack Herer is a great strain for productive pot-heads as a nice steady high awaits. There are legs to its high and just a little bowl of the exceedingly heavy nugs goes a long way in creating an enlightening session. The taste is exceptionally spicy, much like its aroma. Though Jack Herer is predominantly a sativa stone, the buds have an indica structure that's packed with pistils and the bud density does a great job at protecting delicate tri-chomes. Jack Herer's upbeat flavor and flight is perfect for morning wake and bake sessions. Whether you're running off to work afterwards or spending the day around the house, it's a perfect "get stuff done" stone.

JACK JEAN GUY

A private head stash I just had to pick up to explore, Jack Jean Guy blends one of my favorite strains, Jean Guy, with Jack Herer to create an interesting and tasty offspring. My expectations were so high that I was actually pleasantly surprised to find that I wasn't let down by it. Then again, anything influenced by Jean Guy has to be good, right? The exceedingly heavy looking buds appeared beautiful with their flecks of orange trichomes. When the rock solid nugs are busted, Jean Guy's unique floral spiciness rises up and takes over, completely blowing away the lively Jack Herer flavors that ride quietly underneath. The very distinguishable dank has an attention grabbing, uplifting buzz before crashing into a couch-locker. You're going to ride your furniture while your head is in the clouds. Your mind is going to drift, and some stoners are really going to space out and become slack jawed. Jack Jean Guy proved to work excellently on my fibromyalgia symptoms with my pain levels dropping dramatically.

Marijuana Smoker's Guidebook

JACK SKUNK

A pungent skunky smelling sativa, Jack Skunk has a notable nug flavor and an unbelievably introspective "think about your life" effect. This pot allows you to ponder problems in a different perspective. Unfortunately, it doesn't last long enough to become a very deep thinker. The smooth Jack Herer flavors are influenced nicely by Skunk #1 to create a delicious original toke. It's not a rancid Skunk, but a sweet one, and sweet Skunks are not my favorites; I like a rank Skunk flavor with a harsh, eye-watering toke. Jack Skunk does cause some lung expanding cough on the exhale, but not much.

JAS BUD

The first thing you'll notice about this popular Vancouver toke is that Jas Bud impressively sparkles with cannabis crystals. Like some kind of Tiffany diamond, it's very ganja glittery! An indica dominant strain and a heavy resin producer, Cash Crop Ken's Jas Bud (Kish x Burmese) has a unique, but not overpowering floral and earthy aroma. The scent is barely noticeable, but is fruity smooth. When vaporized, Jas Bud starts out with soft floral berry tones then ends with a fairly forceful after bite. It's not as acidic or pineapple tasting as Kish, but way more earth-y smooth from the Burmese parent. The flavor is berry unique and doesn't fall off. Just a little Jas Bud goes far, creating great value for your hard earned cannabis coin. The buzz is mostly a slow moving, rolling stone with excellent mental focus. Fantastic weed for slow, focused, creative activities.

J

Marijuana Smoker's Guidebook

J

JORGE CERVANTES' DIAMONDS

Sparkly, shiny and very pretty to look at, Jorge Cervantes' Diamonds is the perfect addition to an engagement party; just add the ring (and the bong) and you're all set to ask a budbabe to marry you. Not just an impressive looking cannabis strain, JCD has everything stoners want in wicked, wild weed. Jorge's Diamonds has a uniquely soft and sweet floral taste that is really exceptional. It's a totally original tasting, indica-heavy strain with a great soaring, stratospheric zip. This is not a sativa skyrocketing effect; instead JCD has a calm, relaxing, mentally clearing cannabis high. People with chronic pain problems are going to be able to sit in a chair comfortably after a session without becoming mentally dull. Your head is way in the clouds, but your body never leaves the runway.

JUICY FRUIT

These hefty, chunky nugs have a commercial berry tasting toke that isn't as exotic as other types of berry-flavored marijuana available. It's kind of bland and boring. After sampling a wide variety of berry strains, Juicy Fruit doesn't measure up as top notch nug; it's good ganja, but not great grass. In the high category, Juicy Fruit is well balanced between sativa and indica. The strain has an okay body stone and provides some pain relief without any mental fogginess. However, like the gum, its effects are not long lasting. It's a quick surge, but then falls off quickly. Juicy Fruit's heavy and beautiful bag appealing buds make it a commercial cropper for fruity flavored strains. The chances of encountering it on your strain hunt are excellent.

JUSTIN BIEBER KUSH

Kush is about as mainstream as Justin Bieber these days so it doesn't come as much of a shock that someone (in this case Cannabis As Living Medicine in Canada) would market a J.B. Kush. This is just your regular, old world tasting Kush cannabis: nothing too spectacular. The taste is a pure Kush assault with each toke lighting up your taste buds like its namesake's stage show. It's not too overpowering in any department, but not too bland either. The indica stone dropped my chronic pain levels several notches without making me too groggy, as it's an alert active high with wonderful grounding properties. However, like most Kushes, you will enjoy losing track of time after toking it. Kush really has become the Justin Bieber of bud, meaning that whether or not you're interested, it's everywhere. The strain dominates doobie awards and is being bred into everything, like the band with a sound that everyone else decides to copy.

K-TRAIN

Depending on when it's harvested, K-Train will lean towards either a Trainwreck sativa or an OG Kush indica. When it's more sativa, anticipate an exceedingly strong Haze-like spiciness that is just delicious. This was an exceedingly spicy sample with hints of earthy undertones. K-Train has tremendously complex flavors and aromas. My specific sample was a Trainwreck experience; soaring, uplifting, motivational marijuana with pleasant body sensations too. Although my sample was very sativa, the chunky buds were purely indica in their appearance. K-Train is usually more indica dominant, but this sample just happened to be more sativa leaning. The up time is lengthy with the soaring sensation giving way to a groovy, relaxed and mellow chill vibe.

KING'S PURPLE

This strain is a delicious, earthy Kush cannabis combo of
two stellar indica strains, King's Kush and Purple Kush.
There are few noticeable traits from the Purple Kush
side and the pure indica nugs don't release their strong
Kush odor until busted. When you do bust them, the
earthy Kush smells twinkle your nose with their wild,
weedy essence. Buds are loaded down with massive
amounts of trichomes, making King's Purple a Kush
lover's dream. One joint will have many fanatics peacefully dreaming and others losing track of several hours.
Days and nights just melt away after a session of King's
Purple. Besides a great ganja stink and stone, KP is also
an over the top toke of pure Kush greatness. Plenty of
dealers will refer to their wares as King's Purple regardless of whether it's true or not; however, if it's stellar pot,
why not give them the benefit of the doobie doubt?

K

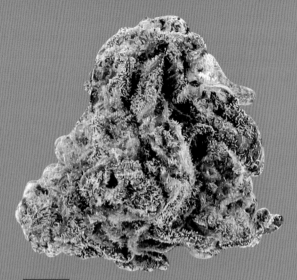

KISH

Cash Crop Ken's husky Kish nugs have an authentic fruity aroma that has hints of blueberry, but also something different that's hard to put your finger on. Kish is an exceptional berry toke that is neither too harsh nor too soft. The best is that its flavor lasts all the way to the end. The indica dominant plant has a strong, slow down meditative stone. Kish quiets my mind and allows me to focus when I'm feeling mentally scattered. After a long hard day, coming home to Kish makes it all better. Your work day stress can be gone as fast you can roll and inhale. Kish is a great kick back, put some tunes on, personal toker time weed. It's an excellent example of a dense and tasty indica.

KUSHBERRY

Anticipate your dense Kushberry nugs making a 'plunk' sound when dropped – they really are that heavy! The firm, dank buds are packed with an incredible amount of powerful Kush goodness. The flavor is slamming OG Kush with soft hints of fruity Blueberry, which is an awesome addition to the Kush genetics. Kushberry has very excellent stoner and medical qualities. Professional potheads will twig to its couch-locking properties that are long lasting, making it perfect pot for a movie night. Kushberry gets you good and stoned, especially when it's ripped in a nice clean bong. Its pain relieving properties are fantastic and make sitting much easier for me. Kushberry is a potent slow-a-stoner-down indica, to the point where new potheads should be peacefully slumbering after a hit or three.

L.S.D.

Barney's Farm's L.S.D. is an amazingly smooth but, of course, trippy stone; a euphoric, creative couch-locker. Your feet are firmly grounded while your head is dancing in the clouds. These astonishingly upbeat qualities mesh perfectly with the soft sedate ones so it doesn't become unpleasant. L.S.D. is great for social functions because cannabis enthusiasts become chatty rather than sleepy; anticipate that the room will get very loud as people become lit up with excitable chatter. It does, however, induce the munchies something fierce. The pumping taste is sharp, but not Skunky, with a delightful hash-like after bite. L.S.D. has an incredible aggressive, sweet, pungent Skunky aroma. Its robust stench gets your stoner senses salivating. Once encountered you will always remember L.S.D. because it has a considerable flashback quality, if there is such a thing: you're trekking around, not having toked some in a while, when your stoner senses become all twigged out in a good way. Barney's Farm created L.S.D. from a combination of an old Skunk #1 and Mazar-i-Sharif to create a weirdly indica dominant strain with plenty of fascinating sativa traits. The longer flowering phenotype has an even spacier stone. Everyone who encounters L.S.D. falls in love and without a doubt it's a creative couch-locker worthy of its name. Psych pot like no other.

L

LA CONFIDENTIAL

There's no confidentiality regarding the fact that DNA Genetics' intense, hunky indica, LA Confidential, is almost perfectly flawless. Nearly everything about this amazing cannabis strain makes it an A-list entry. You will notice an overpowering, coarse, earthy funk with subtle hints of Afghani or Kush lingering just beneath the surface. This cannabis celebrity announces its presence with an exotic, one-of- a-kind aroma. Your senses will tingle in anticipation as you're rolling because buds release an incredible earthy, hash-y richness. LA Confidential's first rip destroys plenty of potheads with its awesomeness. Even for enthusiasts, their regular bong load becomes a one-hitter quitter. Most heads may have problems finishing their regular joints, and doobies will be a resinous gooey mess before you're through. LA Confidential is a downward destroyer so it's important to keep munchies and other important items like phones nearby, because if you need something chances are your couch-locked ass won't be able to travel far after toking.

LAVENDER KUSH

Oh my! Yes, indeed it does smell like real Lavender with hints of Kush. The flowery perfume is overwhelmingly pleasant. It's not a mild odor, but a lovely, extraordinary, excessive lavender stench easily capable of stinking up a room. Lavender Kush does have a deceptive lung tickle, which feels a little strange as something so beautiful smelling shouldn't have harshness; beware that bong rips may cause coughing fits. Points are awarded for having an excellent "if you don't cough, you don't get off" quality. Lavender Kush produces a heavy, thick and deliciously yummy toke while the vibe picks up speed quickly. You'll find yourself suddenly flying, but not going anywhere. You're not locked in place; just feeling inward. The relaxing introspective buzz had me happily staring into space. This is wonderful weed for meditation or other sedate slow activities. Unfortunately, Lavender Kush is currently a private breeder stock making it difficult to find for now.

LEGENDS ULTIMATE INDICA

The first thing you're going to notice about Legends Ultimate Indica is its mellow, slow-you-down stone because it has very little odor and taste. Worst of all, it looks like your standard, run of the mill indica with tight compact buds that do little to distinguish themselves from other indicas. The dull flavors are very smooth and will tickle up your pothead palate in a manner few strains do. However, LUI is very deceiving because the downward stone is where this legendary strain wallops the cannabis competition. Ultimate Indica doesn't make you sleepy; it puts you straight to sleep by cranking you past the "sedate" stage very quickly and heads directly on to bedtime. Too much of this hardy heavy stone and you will wake up some time the next day fully rested and possibly late for work. Many of my writing sessions have ended because the downward slow vibe is so creative zapping; the weedy words would just stop flowing after a Volcano vaporizer canister. Legends Ultimate Indica is wonderful stone-y weed.

L

LEMON AMNESIA

Oh boy, something that may cause forgetfulness. Who doesn't want to forget their problems from time to time with some toking? Lemon Amnesia has excellent astringent, acidic aromas and these loud, lemony smells certainly don't disappoint when it comes to inhaling. My first vapor bag was potent and popping with soaring sativa yumminess. The Amnesia Haze side provides a pleasant, almost trippy stone that goes straight to your dome, making this wonderful weed to smoke before kicking back to watch something very visual like a sci-fi movie. Something with plenty of colors really adds to the Lemon Amnesia vibe. The best thing here is that there are no jittery or uncomfortable soaring side effects, which is something I detest in sativa doobies. I've learned to live with this problem by not over-toking them, but with Lemon Amnesia, this isn't even an issue.

LEMON KUSH

Not the smelliest Kush, but one of the most astringent tasting I've ever come across. The lemon scent isn't very noticeable even when busted into a fine pot powder. Though Lemon Kush may lack a scent, it's easily overlooked because its potency and taste are one step beyond. It's a real lemon zinger that is going to light up your mouth with a fresh sour flavor and explosive Kush undertones. The adorable astringent zest can only be found in citrus tinged cannabis strains. Lemon Kush is mostly an indica strain, making it great for late afternoons or evenings. Reach for Lemon Kush near the end of your day, as it's a sit down and relax kind of stone; I drank a large coffee before my session and still had some problems getting tasks done. My pain levels dropped dramatically, but I also had an unproductive feeling. Lemon Kush is not a choice selection for wake and bakes (duh!), but other than that there's nothing weedy wrong with this zesty, lemon-y fresh toke.

L

LILAC KUSH

The heavenly heavy Lilac Kush holds absolutely nothing back. Her wonderful flowery scent is overpowering with an up time and flavor that are both equally as impressive. The smell is similar to lilacs, making it easily recognizable, but this was a private breeder's creation, so its availability is limited. When I left my stash jar open, this great Kush smelled up my space something fierce, and potheads miles away had to be wondering where that weed dank was coming from. Lilac Kush buds have plenty of trichomes that produce a complex taste that's electric: phenomenal Kush perfumes explode immediately upon inhaling. The taste lingers in your mouth and the dank doesn't fade quickly, hanging around long after a joint has been extinguished. While you're happily buzzing, anticipate the zesty flavor and aroma calling you back for one more. Lilac Kush has an expansive high with endless possibilities and no paranoia, which is especially good considering that, because of how tasty it is, you tend to toke way more than you intend to. I know I did! Lilac Kush is fantastically relaxing and perfect for lazy afternoons where weed napping is possible.

M39

Anticipate straight up solid, dense nugs with little flavor. Unless it's grown correctly – and it almost never is – this strain is to be avoided. M39 has everything a commercial cropper is seeking; fast flowering, weighty, easy to grow nugs with big bud bag appeal. The downside is that it has little to offer the toker, unless grown properly. However, when not produced by cannabis clowns, M39 can be a very enjoyable toke. You will be surprised how good the bud is when grown correctly; I know I am. The astringent taste can be brought out to the point where it makes your face tingle, especially if you exhale through your nose. If it's too acidic – or not cured or flushed properly – your nose will light up like Rudolph the Red Nosed Reindeer. M39's lazy stone is great for people who want to sit in their easy chair totally slack jawed. The best thing about it is that M39 is an affordable pain reliever. Plenty of chronic pain sufferers I know reach for M39 because it is the best relief for both pain and stretched finances.

MANGO

The first hit of Mango is a hardy, heady one and should be packed with ripe melon richness. Mango produces a mind blowing, slightly savory toke worthy of a new vapor bag. The fruity flavors, like Mango's uplifting zippy high, are excessive and exceedingly intense. Mango has a euphoric, energetic effect and is ideal in social settings because of its chatty cannabis high. People who feel a little blue or are suffering from too much winter will really enjoy Mango's mood enhancing effect. Fluffy light green buds have plenty of orange and red trichomes that are covered in crystals. Mango is an excellent addition for any professional pothead's breakfast because a bong rip, joint or vaporizer session will have you flying out the door without a jittery "too much coffee" effect.

MASTER KUSH

The incredible earthy Kush dank busting out of Master
Kush buds lets you know that it's a cut above all others.
MK gets your toker taste buds tingling right away as
they anticipate its succulent, opulent, deep Kush flavors.
Pound for pound, Master Kush nugs are beyond solid,
and are possibly some of the most dense nugs you're
going to come across in your hunt. Even better is the
fact that a small amount goes a long way. However, the
taste and stone is so amazing you're probably going to
toke more than you normally would. Master Kush is best
rolled in a joint because the smoke is creamier in a joint
than as vapor. Long drawn out hauls on joints are a sure-
fire way to feel heavy and rested and, by the end, your
joint will be a resinous, gooey mess. It's a sedate stone,
very mellow and sluggish, that lets you just sink into a
couch and unwind for a good long time. Several seed
breeders offer their own Master Kush, a cross of Hindu
Kush and Skunk.

M

MAX OG KUSH

A fascinating take on a familiar strain, Max OG Kush is a flavorful and phenomenal toke that Kush-loving pot-heads will twig to. The buds create an incredible sluggish feeling that slows down both your body and your mind. Be prepared to roll into bed after toking and be warned that Max OG Kush is not a social stone at all; it's a slack jawed, fall-out-of-your-chair stone. The second and third vapor bags are equally as powerful as the first, with a lung expanding vapor that will for sure cause many cannabis enthusiasts to cough and get off. Max OG Kush doesn't look much different to any of the other OG Kush strains on the market, making it a challenge to say how an enthusiast could differentiate between Max OG and OG Kush when buying.

M

MEDI KUSH

A surprisingly strong Kush tasting strain with an interesting and creative couch-lock, Medi Kush is a combination of two great strains, OG Kush and SAGE, and has some people referring to it as "Kushage" in their cannabis circles. Regardless of what you call it, it's phenomenal, and given its creative roar someone could have given it a better marijuana moniker. However, people with chronic pain problems will really twig to Medi Kush's pain reducing properties, making it easy for med pot people to remember the strain name. Medi Kush really dropped my screaming spine pain and stoners will really enjoy its get-on-up, get-on-your-good-foot high. I was chair dancing! This is feel good ganja, making everything feel alright. The mental soar and pain relief make Medi Kush wonderful weed for pained people, but it's also a great Friday night toke. This strain gives a social stone with confidence boosting properties, perfect for meeting new people.

M

MEDI SAINT

When it comes to relieving pain, Medi Saint is a minor ganja godsend. A chronic pain solving strain, it's some kind of Kush. You'll get exactly what you would expect from commercial Kush; a sedate, stoned, heavy eyelid feeling combined with a spectacular Kush taste. Compressed, packed indica buds break up into beautiful fluff to create great burning joints. Roaches are a resinous mess and anticipate a gooey substance staining your fingers. Medi Saint creates a heavy rich resinous smoke or vapor that is fairly flavorful, but burned when I blew it out my nose. The grounding stone eliminates plenty of hours and it's best to keep necessary items nearby before you start your session because Medi Saint makes it easy to become one with the furniture.

M

MÉNAGE-À-TROIS

Unfortunately, this strain is not as thrilling as the name implies. This private breeder stash was sold to me as a sativa, but it had a flaccid vibe, which is the complete opposite of its branding potential. The dense, chunky and pretty buds had no sativa characteristics at all. Menage-a-Trois is a hybrid, I was told, that leans more sativa than indica. However it was a sedate, slow and sluggish stone with an Afghani wilderness taste. It's a harsh toke lacking any delicateness, with plenty of lung expansion. A lung tickler that some people may have a hard time inhaling, Menage-a-Trois does go the distance in keeping a buzz going.

MOUNTAIN TOP

You'd never get to the top of the mountain inhaling
Mountain Top, an oddly named strain because it makes
you think that it must be a soaring sativa. Instead it's a
slow, sluggish, sedate indica with little toker taste, making it very indistinguishable from other sluggish bland
indica strains. The buds have great bag appeal with
their beautiful red and green coloring. The red trichomes really stand out against the lush green to create
a classic cannabis look and feel, and Mountain Top also
produces an intense foggy vapor bag. However, looks
are deceiving as it's barely above mid range. Think Serious Seeds' Chronic crossed with some kind of wispy
sativa.

MR. NICE x BLUEBERRY

The spicy and fruity aroma from this fascinating cross is really going to bring a smile to your face. Your day will instantly brighten once the buds are busted and become even better once you start inhaling, as the bold flavors give way to a soaring, uplifting high. Mr. Nice x Blueberry buds are exceedingly dense and chunky, especially for a strong sativa. They did break up into powdery dust but still produced a powerful vapor bag of awesomeness. Besides a zippy buzz, I had a serious case of the munchies, so I broke out my favorite munchie solution, which is cereal, while I wrote up a review. Put some tunes on and toke out!

M

NEBULA

Nebula's unique floral smells don't become readily apparent until after it's been busted. Once they are, however, beware! It's capable of stinking up your session space with a pungent yet fruity aroma. Nebula tastes as appetizing as it smells. Anticipate a yummy, firm, fruity burst with a stupendously soft and tasty afterglow. Paradise Seeds created Nebula in 1996 as a mostly sativa variety. The somewhat fluffy, resinous buds twinkle with a ganja galaxy of trichomes. Nebula is uplifting, but not stupidly soaring. You'll get a nice overall mental and body buzz on. It's relaxing, yet you remain functional and mostly in control, making this strain excellent weed for afternoon 4/20 sessions. Nebula is the strain to reach for when there is still work to do (but it's work that can be done with a buzz). It's definitely a daytime strain, not a nighttime toke.

N

NORTHERN SATELLITE

A delicious berry-scented strain, Northern Satellite also has plenty of pine aromatic depth to it. The aroma becomes even bolder once the firm but fluffy buds are busted. The lively smell is very memorable and your taste buds will marvel at how great this marijuana tastes. The Northern Lights influence made this a more enjoyable toke for me than just Blue Satellite on its own. The flavors were more pronounced, long lasting and rich and the smoke tastes so exotic and exquisite you'll end up getting through your stash fast. Northern Satellite is a solid hybrid. Its tender sativa trichomes were well protected by a solid indica structure. The buds have some weight to them, but also retain a lovely softness. There's a little amount of resin and they break up into a fine powder, so beware if you use a coffee grinder for your wake and bake session. It's an awake but body buzzing stone; Northern Satellite made sitting at a computer much easier for me, and the high increased my attention to detail.

NOUVEAU KUSH

"Wow, now that's a really strong Kush" is the kind of response you want to hear when you're puff, puff, passing to your bud buddies. Nouveau Kush will get you positive Kush props from fellow potheads because the buds have a rough Afghani Hindu Kush look and feel that requires a pair of scissors rather than a grinder to break them up. Some strains will just gum up grinders something chronic and this is definitely one of them. The chunky smoke creates a very hardy toke and a heavy, lazy stone. Nouveau Kush will sap all your energy and make you feel exceedingly lethargic. I became a stoner slug and totally anti-social, and I discovered this is perfect pot for personal toking time. I wanted nothing more than to kick back in my easy chair and watch a movie. Nouveau Kush is potent pain relieving reefer or a substantial Kush stone for enthusiasts.

NUKEN

This popular Vancouver pot is packed with a sweet taste and a relaxing but clear-headed crunch. There's no loss of mental activity after a session, making it ideal for a wake and bake smoke. Nuken's moderate zip goes some distance and depending on your commute it might have really mellowed by the time you arrive at work. Many potheads might think Nuken is a sativa, but it's an indica dominant strain with bright, floral aromas and flavors. Something about its very berry, but not fruity taste, makes Nuken feel like a sativa. The solid buds don't pack much of a smell until busted; then they release a subtle smell, but nothing overpowering. Overall, Nuken is an enjoyable and complex toke ideal for rushing through your day.

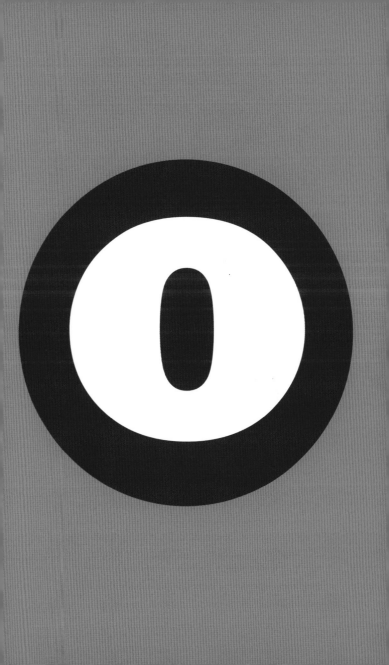

OG KUSH

As you will probably already know, this is the most common cannabis currently available in North America. Every dealer has it, even when they don't – if you know what I mean. OG Kush has exploded in popularity thanks to its amazing qualities, celebrity hype and, obviously, everyone growing it. There was a time when it was difficult to score, and it was only available to the cannabis "in" crowd. Now several seed breeders offer their own version of OG Kush, confusing the marketplace, but also satisfying the demands. The Kush lineage is very expansive. All buds labeled OG Kush will be exceedingly dense and coated in trichomes, even if they're not the real article. They'll make a thud when dropped. Commercial crops (like the one pictured) grown with too much nutrients will still have a distinct Kush odor and taste, which is sour and earthy with hints of pine. Once you've inhaled and experienced this strain you'll consistently recognize it, or at least be able to tell the bud is some kind of Kush. Everything about OG Kush and Kush in general is memorable. The high is uplifting with a strong body buzz. Rookie tokers may green out or become too stoned, so be careful how much you inhale.

OG RASKAL

This strain is very similar looking to traditional OG Kush nugs and it will probably fool even the most professional pothead until busted. OG Raskal (also known as Raskal OG) has hints of pine in its aroma that aren't found in the original Kush strains. You can only find the piney Fire Kush smell when it's busted up, but when you do, expect a wonderful marijuana medley of lemon, Kush and pine. Though the buds look very much like OG Kush, the stone is much different. OG Raskal has amazing couch-locking properties and will surely sit down even the hardiest of tokers. However, there's a slight sativa edge to it that ensures you won't be slumbering. The gentle, uplifting effect is perfect for people who have pain problems who still need to go about their day. It's a shame OG Raskal is more easily accessible on the west coast than in the east because it has serious dank that east coast Kush lovers would adore.

O

OG STAR

OG Star has powerful OG Kush smells and flavors that overpower the Sensi Star side of this unique hybrid in terms of smell and flavor. The enjoyable, crisp taste has an acidic aftertaste that is kind of lemony. After lighting up your toker taste buds, the coarse sensation will linger for a good long while – a very long while, actually. Those who dare to blow through their nose will get a good nostril burn. The rough, hardy, hefty buds lean more towards Paradise Seeds' potent indica (Sensi Star) in appearance and weight. It's a comfortable body relaxer with fabulous mental alertness; a great social high. The stone, like the flavor, also has legs. For many, one toke might send them over the line, but the experienced heads will appreciate how little of this strain is required for a great ride. OG Star shines on.

OG-18

The OG-18 is a standard upon which all Kush strains should be judged. When enthusiasts dream about Kush they should dream only about OG-18. This is the Kush marijuana master! The buds have an incredible amount of heft to them. When broken, they'll release an intense, room-filling smell. Its acidic, lemony aroma will make even the most professional of marijuana enthusiasts drool. OG-18 has a zesty, fuel like flavor that is nothing but pure Kush greatness. This Reserva Privada strain lights up your whole face; your nose, lungs and cheeks will tingle. Your toker taste buds will thank you. It tastes so yum, I took heaping lungfuls that resulted in a massive coughing attack that I knew would happen. I expelled half of my hit before it even hit my lungs, but my taste buds certainly enjoyed it! OG-18 is not a soaring sativa nor is it a sedate stone. Instead, it creates a nice, relaxing chill vibe. An excellent stress reliever that's great for when you come home from work, although your whole day will be spent anticipating the moment you can inhale.

O

OGIESEL

The Cali Connection's efforts at fattening up OG Kush by breeding in some Skunk genetics has created a zealous Kush smell and outlandish stone. Even the smallest amount of OGiesel is going to give you away in public, kind of like a skunk crossing your path. I normally smell like weed, but this had potheads making comments and staring at me on public transit. The wonderful stench is going to stink to high heaven, which is exactly where your mind and body are headed after grinding it up and inhaling your joint. The effects are that of a skyrocketing sativa. The accelerated oomph of OGiesel might be too powerful for some people and it has a stressful anxiety side if you inhale too much. However, it is great for getting stuff done, whatever your stuff may be. The buzz is very active, but I could barely sit still long enough to put words and wisdom down. Distinct sativa buds are packed with plenty of red trichomes; you think they're wispy and lightweight, but upon closer inspection you'll notice they do have some chunkiness. The Cali Connection's OGiesel is an awesome improvement on some already great ganja.

Marijuana Smoker's Guidebook

O

ORANGINA

Wow, the orange coloring to this cannabis strain is almost unreal. Did someone spill orange drink on this dank? It sure looks like it, because the bright Orangina nugs practically glow in an unreal fashion. Orangina has a strong citrus flavor that may bring tears to some stoners' eyes. It's not an artificial orange flavor, but an exceedingly zingy California Orange that tokers will truly want to savor. Best of all is the fact that the taste lingered for what seemed like forever and built up progressively as the session continued. Much to my surprise, Orangina is a sedate indica and not an uplifting sativa. Unfortunately, this mistake put me down after my wake and bake writing session. Not even a double dose of my usual coffee input could save my ass. The cannabis coloring really threw me, making me believe Orangina had to be a sativa. Don't make this mistake if you have to be somewhere in the morning, but if it's your day off toke some Orangina and call it a morning... or a whole day.

P DAWG

The lovely ChemDawg fuel tinge is toned down and perfectly combined with fruity Pineapple Chunk to create a wholly unique strain bursting with bizarre flavors. Potheads who don't like a chemically aftertaste will really like P Dawg, as it is more akin to pineapple expressions than metallic pot pollution. Nugs are much fatter than ChemDawg and have a rough outdoorsy look to them. P Dawg is great for afternoon sessions because it's physically sedate with no mental fogginess. In fact, there's some mental clarity to this cannabis strain that's rarely found in weed. After a session it was really easy to focus on assignments and even on completing mundane office tasks. I'm not sure if this makes P Dawg the cannabis strain of office managers, but it might.

P

PAPAYA

Less fruity smelling than other mango-scented strains, Papaya makes up for this with a powerful indica hit. The smoke is opulent and heavy and the concentrated fruit flavors really overwhelm your taste buds. Papaya's hardy toke is equally matched by its mellow, zone-out buzz. This isn't a social stone, unless you want to chill out in a dark room in the company of fellow cannabis enthusiasts. Papaya's potent, pain-relieving indica stone can easily put down the hardiest of potheads. Immediately after my first vapor bag I began feeling very rested and I zoned out for a while thinking of weedy words to write down. Anticipate a minor munchie attack and have snacks nearby as you might not be able to get up from the couch. Crazily, Papaya buds don't look like they'll pack a potent punch, but they do. You've been fore-warned.

PINK KUSH

Pink Kush is filled with soft scents, earthy flavors and of course, Kushy ganja greatness. The doobies are divine and pain relieving with excellent sedative qualities. This is the one to toke when your pain reaches unbearable levels. For my recreational friends it's a full on couch-locker with very little to no motivating properties. The stone melts away hours and eats up plenty of time, so you're not going to get much done after a Pink Kush session. For some enthusiasts the effects will go long into the day or night, while professional potheads may be able to move after an hour or two. The smells are OG Kush earthy with subtle Purple Kush candy undertones. Be careful not to over grind the dense buds because they'll break up into a fine powder and you'll end up with something that isn't roll ready. Pink Kush is one of my favorite Kushes.

P

PLAIN OLE KUSH

For people who are complaining about too much Kush –
yes, some professional potheads do actually complain
about too much of one kind of marijuana – Plain Ole
Kush is a slap to the stoner scenesters. This strain
harkens back to the days when Kush meant Hindu Kush
or maybe Master Kush. However, Plain Ole Kush doesn't
have a harsh cough and it especially doesn't taste like
any of the California Kushes. Plain Ole Kush's heavy indica nugs produce an opulent, potent Master Kush-like
toke that lasts for hours. The stone is great for kicking
back and soaking in something visual. The fantastic pain
relieving properties are really fab and this is perfect pot
for not getting anything done. Don't be trying to hump a
deadline while toking Plain Ole Kush because you're not
going to complete your project.

Marijuana Smoker's Guidebook

PURPLE D

Anticipate an earthy, Kush stink that isn't too overpowering because Purple D is not the most potent-smelling Kush. However, it packs a powerful punch to the face when ripped in a bong. Purple D is kind of sneaky that way; the smell is underwhelming, but the toke is an overwhelming lung tickler. Plenty of professional potheads will cough and get off because it's a strong indica with awesome downward vibes and body relaxing feelings. Unwind both your mind and your body and you may find yourself sliding out of your favorite chair. The stone is very long lasting and plenty of potheads will wake up the next day feeling refreshed. Purple D buds are mildly ugly looking, but upon closer inspection you'll notice sparkling crystals. Don't let this sly strain fool you: it's a powerful indica.

P

PURPLE DIAMOND

Firm and crystal coated, Purple Diamond buds do indeed have a stoner sparkle to them. When the buds are busted, this potent indica strain releases a fairly strong stink. It's not too overpowering, but it's noticeable. Strangely, the flavor is very mild and not aggressive at all; somehow I thought it would be a taste bud ripper. Purple Diamond scores a real home run, however, in the potency department. The smoke is hardy, heavy and, most importantly, heavenly. Anticipate a sedate effect coming on fast with even the most regular of tokers taking a nap if they're not careful. It's a real insomnia solver! For those who can manage to keep their eyeballs open, Purple Diamond is awesome movie watching weed.

PURPLE GOD

The dark purple, almost black colors of Purple God buds will drop your jaw and have you uttering, "Ganja gawd damn!" The superb purple hues really give these dense buds a majestic feel, but it's difficult to describe Purple God's rather bland taste. The blasé flavor didn't live up to the nugs' superb look. I just expected so much more. However, PG has a deep, mellow, mind unwinding stone and full body relaxing sensations that more than make up for its lack of taste. Purple God is a fantastically powerful indica, requiring just a little bit of it to really put you on easy street. Ensure you turn the lights out immediately after smoking a small joint because a weed nap will be coming on strong. Only the hardiest will endure to smoke another round. Purple God is best enjoyed solo or with a partner immediately before bed.

P

PURPLE KUSH

Purple Kush will be one of the strains you're going to come across most frequently in your hunt. It's a hugely popular toke, but also one of the most mislabeled, so be skeptical; plenty of unnamed nugs simply get labeled as PK. Purple hues are not the only trait to look for; the flavor is an earthy pine with a sweet purple candy aftertaste. The candied sweetness mellows out an initially powerful Kush zing, and you should be ready for the gorgeous candied aftertaste. PK buds will be incredibly compact, chunky, solid and have a big stem. Nugs that have been expertly grown will have purple flecks throughout. This trait is accomplished by dropping grow room temperature in the final week of flowering. Purple Kush is a pure indica with a downward, slack-jawed couch-lock effect. People with pain problems will enjoy PK for its fantastic pain relief. Best of all, it tastes great so it can be toked all day and night without getting tired. Purple Kush slows stoners down to a crawl.

Marijuana Smoker's Guidebook

QUASAR

For many enthusiasts, Quasar's wickedly rank fuel odor is
heavenly. However, not everyone is going to dig its almost
unnaturally foul stench: I know my mom didn't appreciate
me grinding it up in her house. Its bitterness may turn
some off, but for others the severe Diesel odor is unique
to the point where you might not want to stop inhaling
your jar. These are cream cannabis genetics with edgy
flavors that are vibrant and full of depth. The smoke is
rich, thick, and just a little of Quasar's resinous nugs creates an impressive vapor fog. Quasar has an awesome
mellow vibe and a beautifully smooth stone. This weed is
fantastically relaxing; too much will have you snoozing,
but it's serious maxing and relaxing marijuana.

Q

RED DRAGON

Another trippy couch-locker perfect for personal inner journeys or social experiences, Red Dragon has a solid Utopia Haze sativa side that turns it up while your ass remains stuck. Your mind moves forward while you're sitting back grooving to your own ideas. Fascinatingly, Red Dragon is really indica looking, which may throw off tokers who are anticipating a heavy downward buzz. The effects are long lasting and depending on your personal THC tolerance level, could last from 30 minutes to 2 hours. Red Dragon has a similar stone to the L.S.D. marijuana strain, but is even happier and more uplifting. There's a bit more get up and go to Red Dragon than L.S.D., but they're from the same seed company, Barney's Farm.

R

RHAZER

Other than the bright red trichomes packed onto to these hefty nugs, there's very little about Rhazer that showcases its sativa properties. The smell is somewhat noticeable, but it's been dulled by White Rhino to create a fairly light aroma. Something about this strain causes me to cough every time I exhale. Somewhere in the toke lies a spicy zing that could be making Rhazer a lung tickler. However, it's difficult to distinguish because it inhales so smoothly. Rhazer has a mostly smooth soaring effect. Enthusiasts who have problems with zippy weed may find that Rhazer holds steady without becoming jittery. This is great wake and bake bud for people with pain problems or hardworking folks who need to get through a rough morn-

ing or day. There's enough body buzz to provide relief without too much of a couch-lock-ing effect.

RHINO KUSH

Unfortunately this wasn't an overpowering smelling bud. Instead, muted Kush aromas mingled with subtle earthy tones. However, Rhino Kush's stone and taste make it worthwhile weed. Rhino Kush is a very smooth smoke with a complex, lingering flavor of earthy Kush undertones. The narcotic effect is full on the body, but not the brain, creating a superb active mental state. Rhino Kush relaxes your body, but not your mind. People with a high THC tolerance won't become useless, while lightweights will enjoy a mellow but alert experience. Rhino Kush contains plenty of resin-y goodness, which makes for a sticky joint. Whether in a joint, bong or vaporizer, just a little will go far, producing very desirable effects. Dense buds glisten with crystals and tender red trichome hairs protrude outward from within very compact nugs. There are many more tender trichomes on Rhino Kush than White Rhino or OG Kush, making it an excellent combination of the two.

R

ROCK STAR

This marijuana moniker is ganja glamorous, but deservedly so! Rock Star is delicate smelling with plenty of bud plumpness and the soft, enjoyable, expensive scent is very similar to Paradise Seeds' Sensi Star; a wonderful, weedy cinnamon smell. The buds look similar to Sensi Star, but with even more nug density. Bonguru Seeds, founded in 2002, created Rock Star from Sensi Star and Rockbud from Soma Seeds, hence the name, look and smell. Their result is a delicious downward but clear-headed stone. Though billed as an almost complete indica you will think someone slipped in some sativa as there's a strong uplifting mental high happening: you're locked in, but your mind is wandering. Great for creative projects! Awesome for afternoon sessions or for a night on the town as you won't be drowsy. The stone has plenty of depth to it, giving an expansive buzz that continues long after your joint goes out.

RUSSIAN ROCKET FUEL

This cute autoflowering strain has subdued New York
City Diesel petrol scents, which is good news for those
potheads who find the NYCD fuel flavor just too much to
bear. Russian Rocket Fuel doesn't have that over the top
sour flavor because it's been toned down by an unknown indica and Lowryder. The soaring, happy, couch-
locking effect is great for a Monday morning wake and
bake or a smoke for those suffering from depression
that need a mental boost. The mild indica vibe smoothes
out an otherwise soaring sativa high and after an initial
jolt you settle into a steady orbit. Russian Rocket Fuel is
a great private head stash because it's an autoflowering
strain that produces a decent personal supply. You're either going to have to grow it yourself or know someone
who does to find it. However, for people into autoflowering strains, it's well worth the investment.

SAGE

The exceedingly Haze-y spice and sandalwood incense
fragrance emitting from SAGE is truly amazing. The
smell leaps out at you as soon as the stash jar is opened
and the nugs smell so grand you might not want to grind
them up. The spicy smooth taste is a toker's delight with
soft Afghani tones riding a wave of spiciness. Its well-
balanced buzz starts out with a sativa zip before settling
into a nice smooth indica ride. SAGE gives you great
height without leaving your chair. The towering men-
tal/creative couch-lock is deep rooted and ends on a
slow note. Designed to be the best of both weed types,
Sativa Afghani Genetic Equilibrium or SAGE accom-
plishes the task that its name sets down.

S

SENSI STAR

A bold burst of lemon scents, Sensi Star is especially
stinky for a predominantly indica plant. The rock solid
nugs give off an enjoyable sour stench. The smell isn't a
fake sweet sour, but a truly surprising one. Sensi Star's
lemon fresh flavor inhales very hard, even in a vaporizer; your face may contort and contract after exhaling
the lemon pine freshness. Be warned: this is a fantastic
sleepy time toke and only a little is required to truly feel
passive. New potheads may easily green out with good
Sensi Star, as it is extremely robust. The meditative high
massages your mind into an astonishing peacefulness.
This is great ganja, especially for eliminating stressful
days. Sensi Star shines brightly; it's not my favorite, but it
does make me space-y. And who doesn't like to space
out once in a while?

SHARK SHOCK

A heady high with wonderful relaxation vibes, Shark Shock is perfect for a lively afternoon session with friends. There's a slight perfume odor, but nothing to write home about. The uplifting, social zip is influenced by Skunk #1, while the steady, smooth, stress-free buzz comes from White Widow; it starts out quick then slides into a nice steady pace. The buzz is neither too slow nor too quick – it is just right. On the inhale you'll notice a white strain spiciness and a harsh Skunky aftertaste that remains long after your joint has gone out. Shark Shock nugs have some heft to them; they are glittery, sticky and create a rich, resinous and hardy toke. The gooey nugs gummed up my gear as well as the baggy that the buds came in.

Marijuana Smoker's Guidebook

SKUNK #1

With plenty of breeders offering their own version of this venerable cannabis strain, there's little to argue about when it comes to anything labeled Skunk weed, especially considering the stone can either be a sativa or an indica depending on your source. Essentially, if it stinks like a Skunk then it's Skunk #1; a foul stinky strain that hasn't been around as much lately in North America, but used to be hugely popular. I'm talking more than OG Kush popular! The indica is more of a rancid harsh Skunk toke, while sativa Skunks have a more sickly sweetness about them. The stone is just that: you are stoned! Neither too euphoric nor too downward, the effects of this strain are pure textbook. Skunk #1 is one of the first true cannabis hybrids, created by the Sacred Seed Company by mixing a choice Afghani indica with two stellar Mexican and Colombian sativas. As one of the first true stable strains, Skunk has been bred into many, many, different types of cannabis. Somewhere in the lineage of many strain, there is a Skunk. Even to this day when I smell a skunk I try to determine if it's the plant or animal.

S

SOUR CREAM

DNA Genetics' breeding team know that spicy and sour go great together! Sour Cream combines a truly unique Haze spiciness and a Sour Diesel metallic fuel tinge for an utterly awe-inspiring toke. This sativa strain smells absolutely amazing with its incredibly expensive floral aroma. The substantial nugs are clustered with delicate trichomes that produce a mellow uplifting zip. Sour Cream is a very enjoyable, relaxing and mentally alert high. Some sativas make me jittery when I toke too much, but not Sour Cream, probably because there's a strong indica influence to keep me grounded. The strain worked wonders on my fibromyalgia symptoms, probably because it's a sativa leaning hybrid with enough indica in it to manage pain problems. You should note that Sour Cream, despite its name, is not a Cheese strain.

SOUR DIESEL x PURPLE URKLE

The bittersweet Purple Urkle combined with an awe-somely awful Sour Diesel sour taste creates a tasty private head stash. Starts out with a strong and biting bitter taste that then gives way to a sour-ish, but not petrol-like, taste. Moderately dense buds break up beautifully, releasing a wild, weedy odor. Ride your couch to the moon with this powerful hybrid. This strain made sitting in my office chair much more comfortable. Sour Diesel's uplifting mental clarity goes great with the body buzzing and pain-relieving effects of Purple Urkle. Interestingly, this strain ends on a high note, not a sleepy or sedate one. Though you probably won't be able to find this exact cross, you can combine both into a joint for a similar effect and taste.

S

SOUR DIESEL x THAI TANIC

Although it didn't have much of an expansive odor, possessing just subtle hints of sour chocolate, Sour Diesel x Thai Tanic is just delightful in the flavor department. It became expressive once inhaled, and the bitter, dark chocolate-y smoke went down oh so smooth. When it comes to taste you're going to want to inhale this strain all day, if you can find it! The buds broke up beautifully with some stickiness and even a small amount created yummy vapor bags. Expect a clear-headed motivational zip. Unlike some sativa strains with their anxious, paranoid vibe, this stash had a wonderful steady ride. Instead of blasting off quickly, it gently guns you upwards. Beware: it has strong creeper qualities, allowing you to easily overestimate how much to enjoy. Plenty of strains have Sour Diesel in them, and you can see that it's a great breeding plant as evidenced by this unique creation.

SOUR TANG

The sour twinge to this toke is terrific, but Sour Tang is not as acidic or metallic tasting as Sour Diesel. This makes it much easier to inhale for people who want a soaring sativa without the acquired, tangy taste of Sour D. The zip isn't a speedy, physical high, but a mental, up-lifting zing, great for creative or social sessions because your mind is engaged. You'll become chatty or wordy, or you might see things differently. It's a munchies-induc-ing strain and goes great with fruit because the flavors mix exceedingly well. People who have appetite prob-lems should really seek out Sour Tang. This strain makes great morning marijuana because of its fruity aromas, flavors and, most importantly, its get-up-and-go high. Toking Sour Tang made me really want to greet the day with a stoned, happy smile.

S

SPOETNIK 1

Spoetnik 1 skyrockets with very soft and subtle hints of grape-y flavors. The taste can easily be overlooked because it requires finer taste buds to figure it out. You're going to notice and remember Spoetnik's aroma though; she smells like expensive perfume, not like a cheap date. Your nose will be overjoyed. Her aroma might have oversold her taste, leaving it less considered than the pleasant pot perfume. Spoetnik's solid buds create a clear-headed high, but it's not a sativa. Unfortunately, the great couch-locking properties aren't long lasting and like the rocket it's named after, Spoetnik 1 has a quick lift off, but it won't take you to the moon.

SWEET DEEP GRAPEFRUIT

Sweet Deep Grapefruit by Spain's Dinafem Seeds is incredibly balanced. From the flavor to the complex scent to the deep stone, it's an excellent hybrid. SDG is a brilliant blend of Blueberry sweetness and tangy Grapefruit, kind of like Pineapple, but not really. It's not aggressively acidic or berry flavored, but is somewhere in between the two tastes. SDG buds are so gorgeously coated with cannabis crystals that they'll gum up your weed works. They release a soft, fruity, expressive aroma when busted, but generally don't release much of a scent. Nugs have phenomenal bag appeal and make great nug porn. The Sweet Deep Grapefruit high flies deep into the day, but be forewarned: the ending is a crash. I became sleepy as the flight wore off and eventually had to take a nap.

S

SWEET TOOTH

The glorious candied indica taste from Sweet Tooth is very charming. It's a delicious dessert strain that is excellent for after dinner party sessions, but only if you want a chill and relaxed mood. Sweet Tooth's light, fluffy, bright green nugs and pink trichomes create a slow-you-down mode, but it shouldn't be too sedate for professional potheads. I was rocking out, throwing two finger devil horns and generally enjoying the aggressive hard rock stone to Black Sabbath's *I* and Tool's *The Pot* – all while stuck to my chair. Sweet Tooth's delightful flavor and relaxed buzz is good to the very last vapor bag. A highly enjoyable strain that brings back memories of a time before Kush.

SYRUP

You have to love a toke you can almost chew! Syrup has a classic old school '70s Northern Lights taste. It's an opportunity to experience marijuana like your parents or grandparents did when they first inhaled. You will cough and get off! Syrup buds may look a little rough, especially if not given proper attention during the trim, but they're very weighty. When smoking a joint of Syrup anticipate it becoming a sticky, resinous mess to the point where joints release a gooey resin that just pours onto your hand like syrup being applied to pancakes. It's an excellent personal stash strain, but unfortunately only people who grow Syrup will experience it because it's an autoflower.

S

THAI TANIC

A great play on words! Unlike its namesake, Thai Tanic will have you soaring rather than sinking. The Flying Dutchmen have developed a sativa with a fantastic flight time, yet for a sativa it doesn't have a strong noticeable smell at first. After a good sniff, however, you'll be able to detect hints of coffee and chocolate-y ganja goodness. Prepare for a zippy motivational "get on up and go" vibe that will have you bouncing around your session space. This strain also has some mild trippy elements, so people who are used to downward couch-locking Kush strains will find Thai Tanic to be powerful pot. The Flying Dutchmen breeders have taken a long flowering landrace Thai plant and combined it with Skunk #1, with the goal of retaining the Thai's flavors and high while shortening the plant's height and flowering time, and the Skunk #1 fattens out what would otherwise be wispy nugs. Tokers inhaling since the days of the legendary '70s Thai stick may get fond memories of marijuana from their youth. Other potheads will get a small but potent glimpse into pot's past.

T

THE HOG

Bred for stoned potency and heavy yields, The Hog's smell and taste is thankfully not barnyard, but it is very bland. The taste is very boring, which was acceptable in 2002 when TH Seeds first released The Hog but unfortunately, it doesn't really fly these days. Given the flavorful indicas available, it may come up short for finicky potheads who want the whole weedy package. The buds are going to be chunky with excellent bag appeal, and they'll potentially make a plop sound when dropped on your dealer's scale because they are so heavy. Even smallish nugs have an impressive girth to them. Just a little creates an impressive session of hard-to-focus, slack jaw drooling. This strain is not good for social functions, unless you want a room full of stoners incapable of conversation.

THE PURPS

These simply sensational pieces of purple bud sparkled and twinkled in my Volcano vaporizer canister. I was really impressed with the deep purple hues of these hunky buds. The Purps reigns stoner supreme in the highly competitive "gorgeous purple-hued marijuana" category. Enthusiasts are extra harsh on purple strains, often overlooking their impressive Kush flavors. The Purps has a tight taste with sweet Kush hints, and my toker taste buds had memories of Purple Kush. The Purps is a sedate knock out, a pain reliever and excellent grass to unwind with. The long lasting effects range from waking up in a few hours to sleeping right through to the next day, depending on tolerance. Plenty of stoners seek out The Purps as their must-have strain. It is bucket list bud.

T

THE REAL HP

This strain doesn't look or smell like it's going to be good, but The Real HP is packed with delightfully smooth Afghani hashish flavors. These bitter hash tones have an extremely heavy bite to them. The Real HP is deceiving in its looks, and produces a mellow, creeping vibe. The relaxing stone is great for unwinding both your mind and body and you can anticipate layers of stress and tension melting away after every inhale. After a joint, you may discover hours have passed when you thought it was just a few minutes. Hash Plant strains, like this one, used to be very popular before Kush took over. Old school stoners will really twig to this dramatic tasting toke, but sadly it has become scarce as more growers move on to Kush strains. Stoners seeking a taste of Afghanistan without getting imported hash containing camel dung need to discover The Real HP.

T

TRAINWRECK

The slick running Trainwreck will get you off your rails with its soaring zing of a high. Unlike most sativas with their out-of-the-gate zeal, Trainwreck starts slow, chugging up to full speed. Prepare for Trainwreck's creeper toke because if it catches you by surprise, you'll miss your stop and many more thereafter. The chatty, creative zip gives way to a nice relaxing chill. Trainwreck has a quiet, lemony smooth, spicy flavor and its buds are impressively solid, leaning more towards their Afghani indica heritage than sativa Thai. Delicate red trichomes are protected by hefty ganja girth. I was surprised at how many vapor bags Trainwreck actually created. Personally I prefer K-Train with its more lively tastes and highs over Trainwreck's firm flavor and bright grounded buzz.

T

TROPICANNA

An exotic tropical taste with every toke, Tropicanna will slow you down substantially. You're not going to get much done if you toke a doobie of this before attacking your to-do list; it took me plenty of time to finish writing its entry as my mind wandered and I sat there slack jawed. The big buds had substantial girth and plenty of fantastic red trichomes. Just a little will create numerous vapor bags and an incredible effect. Tropicanna has a complex, hot and dry aroma as well as an original, crisp and smooth taste. It goes down nicely, like a tropical drink.

UK CHEESE

There's an absurd amount of bag appeal to these buds. They're absolutely gorgeous to gaze upon and even better in a bong. Exhaling UK Cheese's heavy dank flavors may cause a serious coughing fit: your lungs are expanding while your taste buds try to recover from an acidic assault. UK Cheese was chosen particularly for its musky, harsh, cheesy taste that causes tears from just about everyone who encounters it. It has a memorably pungent and gutsy aroma, but unlike Exodus Cheese with its mountain goat taste, UK Cheese has a more refined zest. It's an indica dominant strain that produces an impressive downward dull thud. I absolutely love it in my Volcano vaporizer! People with chronic pain problems may find UK Cheese's persistent effects to be the medicinal pot they need to solve their woes.

ULTIMATE INDICA

The first thing you're going to notice about Ultimate Indica is its mellow, slow-you-down stone because it has
very little to no noticeable smell. Worst, it looks like your
standard run of the mill indica with its tight compact
buds that do little to distinguish themselves. However,
looks and smell are very deceiving because the buzz is
where the legendary name wallops the cannabis competition. Ultimate Indica cranks it past sedate and onto
bedtime and too much of this hardy, heavy stone will
have you waking up hours later fully rested. Many of my
writing sessions have ended because the indica buzz is
so creatively negative, but my weedy words stopped
flowing completely for hours after a Volcano vaporizer
canister. Overlook the concentrated dull flavors that are
very smooth because LUI sedate vibe is legendary.

U

ULTRA KUSH

These dense buds have a strong, sickly sweet dank that rides on top of an earthy bed of Kush aromas. While toking Ultra Kush you discover that it's a fantastic and original combination of Skunk and Kush flavors that are very noticeable. Anticipate some cough on your exhale because it's a very lung expanding strain. It continues to tickle your lungs long after exhaling. Ultra Kush earns an 'if you don't cough, you don't get off' badge. This Kush had me hacking up a lung then slammed me with a demotivating, sedate stone. Awesome for bedtime bong rips! After toking, the only task you might be able to accomplish is choosing which movie to watch, though I'd recommend doing that before your session. My chronic pain problems are greatly reduced for a while after inhaling Ultra Kush and a joint should happily get most people through a movie.

ULTRA SKUNK

The ultimate classic cannabis stink is Skunk. Pungent,
foul and difficult to disguise, Skunk marijuana was
everywhere back in the days before Kush. Yes, it does
smell like a skunk has crossed your path. Ultra Skunk is
an effort to create the ultimate Skunk strain. The results
are a toke that is softer, easier and less complex than
Skunk #1 – in fact, it's almost too smooth. Ultra Skunk has
less lung expanding coughing fits than traditional
Skunk, which is something I look for in a Skunk strain,
along with a great stink! Anticipate a stellar flight with
plenty of up time and a great creative spring in your
step. There was a time when if you smelled Skunk you
didn't know if it was the animal or the plant.

U

VANILLA KUSH

With every inhale a super smooth, vanilla-tinged Kush yumminess explodes in your mouth. Vanilla Kush's charming flavor creates delicious doobies that pack a powerful, potent and sluggish stone. A small amount creates a chill, relaxing vibe that Barney's Farm lists at an outlandish 22 percent THC. It's no boast; it's believable! Regular size Vanilla Kush joints devastate me and for social occasions mix well with sativa strains to create a chilled but talkative room. The full body aroma of lavender and vanilla should really impress bud babes. You're not going to have to take deep whiffs to determine if it is truly Vanilla Kush because the smell jumps out of the container the moment it's opened. When busted, the buds release an aggressive Kush stench. With its amazing aromas, flavors and stone, Vanilla Kush should really appeal to Kush aficionados, as it's unique enough to distinguish itself from the cluttered field of Kushes.

V

VIPER

A pungent earthy stink, Viper has loud bold flavors that sting your taste buds into stoner submission. The tip of your tongue and roof of your mouth just get hammered by Viper's Kush-like, Cheese-y venom. Best of all is the fact that Viper's flavor doesn't die off: it's good to the last vapor bag and the end of every joint. The stone is a clear-headed indica high, making it perfect for computer work, gaming or other sitting activities that still require mental alertness. Viper has amazing body relaxing qualities and worked wonderfully at reducing my fibromyalgia symptoms. It's great for afternoon sessions and is perfect pot for socializing. Buds have a heft to them, are rough looking and are packed with trichomes. Not for the faint at heart or potheads with weak sensibilities.

WAPPA

Another classic-smelling cannabis strain, Wappa has a traditional Amsterdam dank about it. Professional pot-heads who haven't experienced Wappa before should be able to distinguish it clearly as pot straight from Amsterdam because it has that unmistakable 'dam stink. The strong body buzz doesn't prevent people from getting tasks done, but there's an insightful introspective high going on too, which is a common trait in Amsterdam cannabis. Wappa is great outdoor toking weed because you can sit in a park or go for a hike, blaze a joint, then just peacefully chill. You have to find the perfect spot in advance, though, because the chill body buzz will have you lying in the grass for hours. Wappa's not really a so-cial talkative stone, but for intimate sessions it's a solid cannabis choice.

W

WATERMELON

Lovers of fruity strains rejoice! Watermelon does indeed smell and taste like a slice of melon. However, it's not like an actual piece of fruit – more like a candied flavored fruit, making it super yummy! The nugs give off a great ganja stink and many enthusiasts will be able to recognize its fruity ganja goodness from Watermelon's aroma alone. This strain is a great summertime toke with a motivational get outside moderate body buzz. It provides plenty of pain relief without interfering with tasks. Enthusiasts will dig smoking a doobie and then going about their day with a nice heady high. I was really impressed with the number of vapor bags Watermelon produced. It's a spectacular strain and weedy welcome addition to the growing number of fruity strains. Soon enthusiasts may regard it as wonderful as Grapefruit or even the legendary Blueberry.

WHITE BUBBLEGUM

The fantastic floral tones of white marijuana are beautifully combined with sweet bubblegum flavors to create
a wholly unique taste in this strain. White Bubblegum
nugs are gorgeous and exceedingly compact, but
they're heavy to the point of impressiveness. The aromas
just jump after the buds are chopped and I learned that
just a little White Bubblegum produces a potent, candy-
tasting vapor bag or joint. Of course, it goes great in a
clean and iced bong, too! The indica stone is mostly
downward, body and mind relaxing in the slide-out-of-
your-chair-drooling kind of way. Be prepared, because
White Bubblegum blows your pot panties off and you
may wake up from a wonderful weedy nap hours later.
Passing out in a chair or couch is a strong possibility
after a session with this great strain.

WHITE DWARF

A unique, delicious and tasty toke that is unfortunately difficult to discover, White Dwarf is an autoflowering strain that produces a personal stash ensuring that you either have to grow your own or know the person who did. White Dwarf has a spicy flavor and an attractive perfume. It's very spicy and once ground, you're really going to notice its powerful aromatic properties that are extremely similar to White Widow. Fans of White Widow may have a soft spot for this small plant. The high is not ideal for a wake and bake, but is excellent for after work or prime time puffing. It will slow you down to the point where too much may have you tapping out and napping. A sleep-solving indica, White Dwarf has buds rich with white frosting and packing fantastic toking properties.

WHITE RHINO

White Rhino's heavy buds release an earthy stink with hints of White Widow's wonderful uniqueness that makes me tingle. The aromas and heavy tastes are greatly muted compared to WW so you won't confuse the two! White Rhino buds are heavier, compact and tougher appearing (because it's more indica dominant) than other White strains. White Rhino was created from a pedigree of excellent genetics and is a perfect complement to its mom. It has more sedate properties than White Widow and fantastic couch-locking qualities. White Rhino is mildly narcotic, making it great for evening sessions. If you're toking in the afternoon be prepared to go down for the cannabis count, because that's what I had to do. White Rhino puts your brain in a mentally sluggish state.

W

WHITE RUSSIAN

White Russian is a gorgeous, sweet and floral smelling strain that packs a potent, soaring sativa, stress-relieving stone. Having been around for some time, White Russian's aroma is best described now as classic Amsterdam. It is dank like all great ganja and the harsh, heavy and resinous taste is going to really excite professional potheads. White Russian leans more towards AK-47 than spicy White Widow. The nugs are weighed down with an incredible amount of crystal development that results in a beautiful, euphoric high. It's wonderful weed to come home to after a long day at your job because its high is so relaxing but not dulling. White Russian's uplifting buzz complements plenty of active and outgoing activities. I'm a huge fan of White marijuana strains to treat my fibromyalgia symptoms and White Russian is possibly one of the best at managing my illness.

WHITE WIDOW

A true cannabis champion, White Widow's lively spiciness has garnered a legendary reputation. The aroma is close to peppery and will prickle a well-trained toker's nose. Best of all, White Widow's voluptuous, unique smell exactly matches its flavor. Anticipate a black pepper and cinnamon explosion with every inhale and a pleasant body-relaxing buzz. However, there's no dullness. Instead, White Widow has an alert, active quality, making it wonderful for intense mental activity. You're going to be chilled and relaxed, but focused. This is excellent pot for social functions. White Widow is the mother of a long lineage of White marijuana strains and it continues to be a staple on many Dutch coffeeshop menus. A whole sub category of cannabis is dedicated to White strains and they're my favorites; White Widow, White Rhino, and Great White Shark. I'm always on the hunt for great White strains.

WILLY JACK

Anticipate a surprisingly soft but zealous toke from Willy Jack. This is an indica to write a blog about as it has a taste very similar to Williams Wonder with some wonderful bits of Jack Herer marijuana spiciness thrown in. Willy Jack is an easy-to-inhale strain; possibly too easy, because it expands in your lungs something fierce. It goes down smooth then hits hard like a hockey body check or a French Canadian accent. It's mind-wandering weed; you're daydream tripping, getting easily distracted, but not really going anywhere. No tasks are getting done. Strangely complex like poutine, but rest assured: this is willy, willy good weed.

YODA

These Orange Diesel x OG Kush seeds were gifted by an online friend who goes by the screen name Yoda. Out of my five beans I was only able to score one female. Out of my five beans I was only able to score one female, but it was a fantastic, fun, sturdy female to grow, and it ultimately turned heads when toked. The strong Kush scents stank up big rooms and potheads immediately noticed when a jar of Yoda was opened. Professional potheads will notice an underlining Orange Diesel aroma, and, when inhaled, this scent becomes a delightfully strong, acidic aftertaste that lit up my senses something superb. Yoda is a sativa-leaning strain that has a mentally active high with couch-locking pain relieving properties. Sadly, not knowing what to expect and not having space to keep mother plants I did this strain as a one off and really regret it because Yoda is otherworldly. After a session you truly are filled with the force.